National Park Service Camping Guide

Published by:

Roundabout Publications
PO Box 19235
Lenexa, KS 66285

800-455-2207

www.TravelBooksUSA.com

Published by:

Roundabout Publications
PO Box 19235
Lenexa, KS 66285

Phone: 800-455-2207
Internet: www.TravelBooksUSA.com.

Library of Congress Control Number: 2012948583

ISBN-10: 1-885464-43-6
ISBN-13: 978-1-885464-43-9

Table of Contents

Introduction

The National Park Service

On August 25, 1916, President Woodrow Wilson approved legislation creating the National Park Service, a new federal bureau in the Department of Interior. Its responsibility was to protect the 35 national parks and monuments then managed by the department and those yet to be established. Today the National Park Service is made up of nearly 400 units covering more than 84 million acres.

About This Book

America's national parks offer a variety of camping experiences, whether it's in a tent in the backcountry or in your RV parked at a campsite with electric hookups. This book describes the camping opportunities available at more than one hundred National Park Service areas. It not only includes national parks but national seashores, national monuments, national recreation areas, and much more.

Each state chapter begins with a list of National Park Service areas within that state. Each is numbered and identified on a map.

Details for each park include contact information, a brief description of the park including any entrance fees that may be charged and the location of visitor centers. Visitor centers have free maps, brochures, and park rangers available to answer your questions.

Campground information for each park includes directions, season of operation, number of sites, and cost per night. You'll also find a list of amenities and facilities available such as restrooms, dump stations, showers, and more. RV length limits, if known, are provided as are length of stay restrictions. (See Appendix E for more information about RV length limits.)

Additional Information

Be sure to look at the appendices for additional information about the National Park Service. In Appendix A you'll find information about America the Beautiful passes. Appendix B describes the various designations assigned to National Park Service areas such as national parks, national monuments, national recreation areas, etc. In Appendix C you'll find information about visiting parks with your pet. Appendix D is a list of National Park Service areas where camping is free. Appendix E is a convenient list of campgrounds that can accommodate RVs.

Alaska

1   Denali National Park & Preserve
2   Gates of the Arctic National Park & Preserve
3   Glacier Bay National Park & Preserve
4   Katmai National Park & Preserve
5   Kenai Fjords National Park
6   Klondike Gold Rush National Historical Park
7   Kobuk Valley National Park
8   Lake Clark National Park & Preserve
9   Wrangell-Saint Elias National Park & Preserve

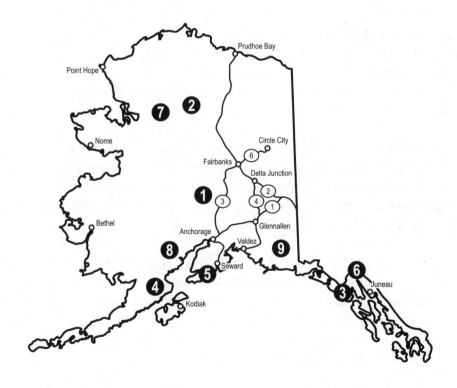

Denali National Park & Preserve

PO Box 9
Denali Park, AK 99755
Phone: 907-683-2294

Denali National Park and Preserve is home to 20,320-foot Mount McKinley, North America's highest peak. Established in 1917 as Mount McKinley National Park, the park was originally designated a wilderness area. In 1980 it was incorporated into Denali National Park and Preserve. The park encompasses over six million acres. Private vehicle access is restricted to the first 15 miles of Denali Park Road. To travel farther into the park, shuttle and tour bus services are available. Bicycles are permitted along the Park Road. The entrance fee is $10 per person.

Park Activities
✓ Auto Touring
✓ Biking
Boating
✓ Camping
✓ Climbing
✓ Fishing
✓ Hiking
Horseback Riding
✓ Hunting
✓ Snow Skiing
Swimming
✓ Wildlife Viewing

Information is available from two visitor centers. Denali National Park Visitor Center is 1.5 miles inside the park and is open 8am to 6pm, mid-May to mid-September. Eielson Visitor Center is at mile 66 of Denali Park Road and is open 9am to 7pm, June to mid-September; it can only be reached by shuttle bus.

There are six campgrounds within the park. Camping is limited to 14 days per year. Reservations are accepted for sites in Riley Creek, Savage River, Taklanika, and Wonder Lake; call 800-622-7275. A one-time reservation fee per campsite is charged. If you do not have advance reservations, plan to camp outside the park when you first arrive. There may be a two-night wait for a campsite within the park.

Backcountry camping requires a permit, available at the Backcountry Information Center near the park entrance. Advanced reservations are not available. Allow one hour for the permit process. All areas require the use of bear resistant food containers, available free with your backcountry permit.

Igloo Creek: located near mile 35 of Denali Park Road, open mid-May to mid-September, 7 tent-only sites, $9 per night, access by shuttle bus only, no potable water, vault toilets are located near the entrance. Pets are not permitted.

Riley Creek: located near park entrance, open all year, 147 sites, $22 to $28 per night ($14 per night for tent-only sites), 40-foot RV length limit, limited facilities September to May, flush and vault toilets, water. A general store, showers, laundry, and dump station are nearby. Camping is free mid-September to mid-May. Pets are permitted.

Sanctuary River: located at mile 23 of Park Road, open mid-May to mid-September, 7 tent-only sites, $9 per night, accessible only by shuttle bus, vault toiles, no potable water, no open fires - campstoves only. Pets are not permitted.

Savage River: located at mile 13 of Park Road, open mid-May to mid-September, 33 sites, $22 to $28 per night, 40-foot RV length limit, potable water, flush and vault toilets available. Pets are permitted.

Teklanika River: located at mile 29 of Park Road, open mid-May to mid-September, 53 sites, $16 per night, 40-foot RV length limit, potable water and flush toilets available. Pets welcome. If you drive your vehicle or RV to the campground, a three-night stay is required. If you use the bus service to reach the campground, there is no minimum number of nights you must stay.

Wonder Lake: near mile 85 on Park Road, open early June to mid-September, 28 tent sites, $16 per night, access by shuttle bus only, potable water and flush toilets available, no open fires - campstoves only. Pets are not permitted.

Gates of the Arctic National Park & Preserve

PO Box 30
Bettles, AK 99726
Phone: 907-692-5494

Gates of the Arctic National Park and
Preserve encompasses nearly 8.5 million
acres of pristine wilderness in Alaska's
Brooks Range. The park is made up of
several elements including the national
park, national preserve, wilderness, six
Wild and Scenic Rivers, and two National
Natural Landmarks. It is primarily
inhabited by caribou, Dall sheep, wolves,
grizzly and black bears. The park receives
around 10,000 visitors annually in search
of a unique wilderness experience. There
are no entrance fees. All visitors are
expected to participate in a free backcountry orientation program.

Park Activities
Auto Touring
Biking
✓ Boating
✓ Camping
✓ Climbing
✓ Fishing
✓ Hiking
Horseback Riding
✓ Hunting
✓ Snow Skiing
Swimming
✓ Wildlife Viewing

Access to the park is by air; scheduled air taxis from Fairbanks serve
Anaktuvuk Pass, Bettles, and Coldfoot. Bush charters are available from
Bettles and Coldfoot into the park. Travelers to Anaktuvuk Pass can hike
into the park.

Information is available from the Bettles Ranger Station, which is open
8am to 5pm seven days a week from mid-June through September. The
rest of the year it is open Monday through Friday from 8am to noon
and 1pm to 5pm. A visitor center is also located in Coldfoot that is open
Memorial Day to Labor Day. There are no visitor centers or facilities of
any kind within the park.

There are no campgrounds, roads, established trails or other maintained
facilities within the park. Wilderness camping in the arctic requires
special care. Visitors must be well prepared and self sufficient. Wilderness
skills are essential. Be prepared for emergencies and radical changes in
the weather; it can snow at any time of the year. Always carry enough
food for extra days because inclement weather can delay air service.

Glacier Bay National Park & Preserve

PO Box 140
Gustavus, AK 99826
Phone: 907-697-2230

Glacier Bay National Park and Preserve is in southeast Alaska. It contains over three million acres of snow-capped mountains, freshwater lakes, and coastal beaches. The park was first established as a National Monument in 1925 and a Park and Preserve in 1980. More than 400,000 visitors a year come to this beautiful park. There is no entrance fee.

Information is available from the Glacier Bay Visitor Center, which is located on the second level of the Glacier Bay Lodge in Bartlett Cove. The center is open late May to early September. Exhibits illustrate the park's natural and cultural history. Park rangers offer evening programs and films in the auditorium.

Park Activities

Auto Touring
Biking
✓ Boating
✓ Camping
Climbing
✓ Fishing
✓ Hiking
Horseback Riding
✓ Hunting
Snow Skiing
Swimming
✓ Wildlife Viewing

There is one campground in the park. All campers are required to attend a free 30-minute orientation offered on schedule at the Bartlett Cove Visitor Information Station. Visitors can obtain a backcountry camping permit and check out a bear-resistant food canister at the information center.

> **Bartlett Cove**: located about one-quarter mile by trail from the main dock, open May through September, 35 campsites, no fee is charged but a permit is required, warming shelter, outhouses, bear-resistant food storage, 14 day maximum stay.

Katmai National Park & Preserve

PO Box 7
King Salmon, AK 99613
Phone: 907-246-3305

Katmai National Park and Preserve is
known for volcanoes, brown bears, fish,
and rugged wilderness. It's also the site
of the Brooks River National Historic
Landmark, which contains the highest
concentration of prehistoric human
dwellings in North America. The 4.1
million acre park is accessible only by boat
or plane, yet more than 50,000 visitors
come to this park each year. Katmai was
designated a National Monument in
1918 and a National Park in 1980. The

Park Activities
Auto Touring
Biking
Boating
✓ Camping
✓ Climbing
✓ Fishing
✓ Hiking
Horseback Riding
✓ Hunting
✓ Snow Skiing
Swimming
✓ Wildlife Viewing

park's headquarters is in King Salmon, about 290 air miles southwest of
Anchorage. Several commercial airlines provide daily flights into King
Salmon. No entrance fee is charged.

A common destination for most visitors is Brooks Camp, about 30 air
miles from King Salmon. All visitors to Brooks Camp are required to
attend the Brooks Camp School of Bear Etiquette offered at the visitor
center. Peak season for viewing brown bears is late June through July and
in September.

There is one campground withinin the park. The campground is set
up for 60 campers to share 18 campsites. Backcountry camping is also
permitted.

> **Brooks Camp**: open June to mid-September, 18 sites, $12 per
> person per night, advance reservations and fee payment required
> (877-444-6777), drinking water, vault toilets, fire rings, picnic
> tables, bear-resistant food storage. Showers available at Brooks
> Lodge (fee charged).

Kenai Fjords National Park

PO Box 1727
Seward, AK 99664
Phone: 907-224-0500

Kenai Fjords National Park is southwest of Seward in south-central Alaska. It encompasses nearly 608,000 acres of rugged, pristine land. The fjords are long, steep-sided, glacier-carved valleys now filled with ocean water. Beyond the coastline, mountains rise dramatically. The park contains much of the 700-square mile Harding Icefield, some 35 miles long and 20 miles wide. Exit Glacier spills off the icefield and is popular with visitors because it can be reached by road. There is no entrance fee charged.

Park Activities

Auto Touring
Biking
✓ Boating
✓ Camping
Climbing
✓ Fishing
✓ Hiking
Horseback Riding
Hunting
Snow Skiing
Swimming
✓ Wildlife Viewing

A visitor center at 1212 4th Avenue in Seward offers exhibits, maps, publications, and other information. It is open daily 8:30am to 7pm, Memorial Day through Labor Day. Information is also available from the Exit Glacier Nature Center, which is open daily 9am to 8pm, Memorial Day weekend through Labor Day.

There is one campground and two public use cabins within the park. Reservations are required for cabin rental, call 866-869-6887 for more information.

Exit Glacier: 12 walk-in tent sites, free, central food storage, cooking and dining shelter, potable water, pit toilets. Sites are available on a first-come, first-served basis; reservations not accepted. There is a 14-day stay limit. Pets are prohibited in campsites.

Klondike Gold Rush National Historical Park

PO Box 517
Skagway, AK 99840
Phone: 907-983-2921

Klondike Gold Rush National Historical
Park is in southeast Alaska in Skagway,
about 96 air miles north of Juneau. It
celebrates the Klondike Gold Rush of
1897-98 through 15 restored buildings
within the Skagway Historic District.
The park also preserves a portion of the
Chilkoot and White Pass Trails and the
Dyea Townsite at the foot of Chilkoot
Trail. A permit is required to hike the U.S.
and Canadian portions of the Chilkoot
Trail. There is no entrance fee.

Park Activities

Auto Touring
✓ Biking
✓ Boating
✓ Camping
Climbing
✓ Fishing
✓ Hiking
✓ Horseback Riding
Hunting
✓ Snow Skiing
Swimming
✓ Wildlife Viewing

Information is available from the visitor center inside the restored
railway depot building at Broadway and Second Avenue. The center is
open Monday through Friday, 7:30am to 7pm (8am to 6pm weekends),
from early May to late September.

There is one campground available to visitors.

Dyea: located nine miles from Skagway near the old townsite of
Dyea, open when free of snow, 22 rustic sites, $10 per night, fire
rings, picnic tables, pit toilets, no hookups, visitors are advised to
bring drinking water and firewood. Reservations not accepted;
sites available on a first-come, first-served basis.

Kobuk Valley National Park

PO Box 1029
Kotzebue, AK 99752
Phone: 907-442-3890

Kobuk Valley National Park preserves approximately 1.7 million acres of land in northern Alaska. Contained within the park is the Great Kobuk Sand Dunes, a 25-square mile area of shifting sand dunes where summer temperatures can exceed 90 degrees. Another attraction is the slow-moving and gentle Kobuk River, which is popular for fishing, canoeing, or kayaking. Access to the park is by air. Commercial airlines provide service from Anchorage to Kotzebue or Fairbanks to Bettles. Visitors may then fly to the park with various air taxi operators. No entrance fee is charged.

Park Activities

Auto Touring
Biking
✓ Boating
✓ Camping
Climbing
✓ Fishing
✓ Hiking
Horseback Riding
Hunting
Snow Skiing
Swimming
✓ Wildlife Viewing

Information is available from the Northwest Arctic Heritage Center in Kotzebue. From June through September, the center is open 8:30am to 6:30pm, Monday through Friday, and 10:30am to 6:30pm on Saturday; closed on Sunday.

Visitors to this remote park must be well prepared and self sufficient. Wilderness skills are essential; you should spend some time studying topographic maps of the area. There are no roads or established trails within the park and no developed camping areas. Tundra and river bars are often used as campsites. Kobuk Valley National Park contains many unmarked parcels of private land, check with the park's headquarters for more information.

Lake Clark National Park & Preserve

Headquarters
240 W 5th Ave Suite 236
Anchorage, AK 99501
Phone: 907-644-3626

Lake Clark National Park and Preserve is in south-central Alaska. It contains more than four million acres of land, stretching from the shores of Cook Inlet, across the Chigmit Mountains, to the tundra covered hills of the western interior. Around 6,000 visitors come to this park each year. Numerous lakes and rivers offer excellent fishing and wildlife viewing opportunities. There is no road access to the park; a one to two-hour flight from Anchorage, Kenai or Homer provides access to most points within the park. There is no entrance fee.

Park Activities

Auto Touring
Biking
✓ Boating
✓ Camping
✓ Climbing
✓ Fishing
✓ Hiking
Horseback Riding
✓ Hunting
✓ Snow Skiing
Swimming
✓ Wildlife Viewing

A visitor center is in Port Alsworth on the shores of Lake Clark. It is open 8am to 5pm, Monday through Friday, year-round. The visitor center is also open on Saturdays in June, July, and August (8am to 5pm). Exhibits and information about the area are provided.

There are no roads within the park. A 2½-mile trail to Tanalian Falls and Kontrashibuna Lake is accessible from the town of Port Alsworth. There are no developed camping areas within the park but backcountry camping is permitted; no permit is required. Visitors that plan on backcountry camping should be well prepared and self sufficient. Wilderness skills are essential.

Wrangell-Saint Elias National Park & Preserve

PO Box 439
Copper Center, AK 99573
Phone: 907-822-5234

This 13.2 million acre park is located in southeast Alaska. Here, the Chugach, Wrangell, and Saint Elias mountain ranges converge. The park contains America's largest collection of glaciers and mountains above 16,000 feet. Mount Saint Elias, at 18,008 feet, is the second highest peak in the United States. Around 40,000 visitors come to the park annually in search of a unique wilderness experience. There is no entrance fee.

Park Activities

- ✓ Auto Touring
- ✓ Biking
- ✓ Boating
- ✓ Camping
- ✓ Climbing
- ✓ Fishing
- ✓ Hiking
- ✓ Horseback Riding
- ✓ Hunting
- ✓ Snow Skiing
-   Swimming
- ✓ Wildlife Viewing

Visitor information is available from the park's headquarters, which is located at mile 106.8 on Richardson Highway. It remains open daily from 9am to 6pm in the summer and 9am to 4pm the rest of the year. Information is also available from the Kennecott Visitor Center (open Memorial Day through Labor Day) and three ranger stations.

There are no formal park service campgrounds. Many visitors simply make camp on public land along the McCarthy and Nabesna Roads. On private land within the park boundaries, and along area highways, there are commercial businesses that offer camping and lodging. Backcounty camping is also permitted.

There are 14 backcountry cabins available for public use on a first-come, first-served basis. Users should not expect amenities or furnishings of any kind. Most cabins are accessible only by aircraft.

Arizona

1   Canyon de Chelly National Monument
2   Chiricahua National Monument
3   Glen Canyon National Recreation Area, see Utah
4   Grand Canyon National Park
5   Grand Canyon - Parashant National Monument
6   Lake Mead National Recreation Area, see Nevada
7   Navajo National Monument
8   Organ Pipe Cactus National Monument
9   Petrified Forest National Park
10 Saguaro National Park
11 Sunset Crater Volcano National Monument

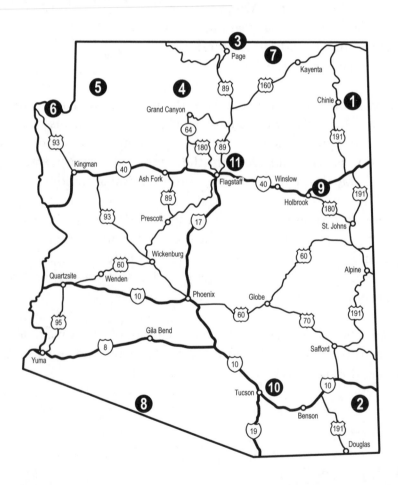

Canyon de Chelly National Monument

PO Box 588
Chinle, AZ 86503
Phone: 928-674-5500

> ## Park Activities
>
> ✓ Auto Touring
> Biking
> Boating
> ✓ Camping
> Climbing
> Fishing
> ✓ Hiking
> ✓ Horseback Riding
> Hunting
> Snow Skiing
> Swimming
> Wildlife Viewing

Canyon de Chelly National Monument is in the Navajo Reservation three miles east of Chinle and 200 miles northeast of Flagstaff. The nearly 84,000-acre park contains ruins of Indian villages constructed between 350 and 1300 A.D. The park remains open all year. No entrance fee is charged. To drive on the canyon bottom requires a four-wheel drive vehicle, a Park Service permit, and hiring an authorized Navajo guide. Hiking within the canyon requires a permit and an authorized Navajo guide, except along the 2.5-mile White House Ruins Trail.

Information is available from the Canyon de Chelly Visitor Center, located three miles east of US 191 in Chinle. The visitor center is open daily all year from 8am to 5pm (except Christmas Day) and has exhibits featuring the cultural history of the area.

There is only one campground within the park, which is managed by the Navajo Parks and Recreation Department. All campsites are available on a first-come, first-served basis; reservations are not accepted. Backcountry camping is permitted with an authorized guide.

> **Cottonwood**: located near the visitor center, 90 sites, $10 per night, picnic tables, grills, no hookups, 40-foot RV length limit, drinking water, flush toilets, dump station, limited facilities in winter.

Chiricahua National Monument

12856 E Rhyolite Creek Rd
Willcox, AZ 85643
Phone: 520-824-3560

Chiricahua National Monument is in southeast Arizona about 36 miles southeast of Willcox and 120 miles southeast of Tucson. The park preserves 12,000 acres of the Chiricahua Mountains and unusual rock formations. An entrance fee of $5 per person is charged.

Information is available from Chiricahua Visitor Center located two miles from the monument entrance. It remains open all year from 8am to 4:30pm (closed Thanksgiving Day and Christmas Day) and has audiovisual programs, exhibits, and books for sale.

Park Activities
✓ Auto Touring
Biking
Boating
✓ Camping
Climbing
Fishing
✓ Hiking
Horseback Riding
Hunting
Snow Skiing
Swimming
✓ Wildlife Viewing

There is only one campground within the monument. Campsites are available on a first-come, first-served basis; reservations are not accepted. Backcountry camping is not permitted. There is no food service, gasoline, or lodging within the monument. Supplies can be obtained from nearby communities.

Bonita Canyon: open all year, 22 sites, no hookups, $12 per night, 29-foot RV length limit, restrooms with flush toilets, water, picnic tables, no showers, 14 day stay limit.

Grand Canyon National Park

PO Box 129
Grand Canyon, AZ 86023
Phone: 928-638-7888

Grand Canyon National Park is in northern Arizona. It encompasses 277 miles of the Colorado River and 1.2 million acres of land. Nearly five million people visit the park annually; visitation is highest in spring, summer, and fall. Reservations for camping and lodging are essential during this time. At the entrance station you will receive an informative paper detailing parking areas, ranger programs, and visitor facilities. The entrance fee is $25 per vehicle.

```
┌─────────────────────────────┐
│       Park Activities       │
│  ─────────────────────────  │
│  ✓ Auto Touring             │
│  ✓ Biking                   │
│  ✓ Boating                  │
│  ✓ Camping                  │
│    Climbing                 │
│  ✓ Fishing                  │
│  ✓ Hiking                   │
│  ✓ Horseback Riding         │
│    Hunting                  │
│    Snow Skiing              │
│    Swimming                 │
│  ✓ Wildlife Viewing         │
└─────────────────────────────┘
```

There are four visitor center locations within the park. The Grand Canyon Visitor is on the South Rim by Mather Point and is open daily from 8am to 5pm. Verkamp's Visitor Center remains open from 8am to 7pm in spring. Desert View Vicitor Center is 25 miles east of Grand Canyon Village on the South Rim; it is open daily from 9am to 5pm. The North Rim Visitor Center is open mid-May to mid-October from 8am to 6pm daily.

There are three developed campgrounds managed by the National Park Service and one managed by a concessionaire. Backcountry camping is available and requires a permit. There is a $10 fee for the permit plus an additional fee of $5 per night, per person. A dump station is located adjacent to Mather Campground and Trailer Village (closed during winter months).

Desert View: 25 miles east of Grand Canyon Village on the South Rim, open mid-May through mid-October, 50 RV and tent sites, seven day maximum stay, $12 per night, no hookups, 30-foot RV length limit. Reservations not accepted. Pets permitted.

Mather: in Grand Canyon Village on the South Rim, open all year, 318 RV and tent sites, no hookups, 30-foot RV length limit, seven day maximum stay, reservations strongly recommended mid-March through November (call 877-444-6777), reservations may be made up to five months in advance, $18 per night April through November, $15 per night December through March (reservations not needed; first-come, first-served). Shower and laundry facilities nearby. Pets permitted.

Trailer Village: concession-operated campground adjacent to Mather Campground, open all year, 78 RV sites, $35 per night, reservations recommended (888-297-2757), full hookups (30 and 50-amp electrical service), 50-foot RV length limit, seven day maximum stay, showers and laundry facilities nearby. Pets are permitted.

North Rim: located off AZ 67 near North Rim, open mid-May to mid-October, 81 RV and tent sites, $18 to $25 per night, no hookups, dump station available, seven day maximum stay, reservations strongly recommended (877-444-6777), coin-operated showers and laundry are nearby. Pets are allowed.

Grand Canyon - Parashant National Monument

345 E Riverside Dr
St. George, UT 84790
Phone: 435-688-3200 or 435-688-3246

Park Activities
Auto Touring
Biking
Boating
✓ Camping
Climbing
Fishing
✓ Hiking
Horseback Riding
Hunting
Snow Skiing
Swimming
✓ Wildlife Viewing

Parashant National Monument is jointly managed by the National Park Service and Bureau of Land Management. The monument is located in the northwest corner of Arizona. It is a vast land of open, undeveloped space. Monument access is by dirt roads with no visitor services available. There is no entrance fee.

Information is available from the Interagency Information Center located in the lobby of the BLM office in Saint George, Utah. The center has maps, field guides, books, and other items. Personnel are available to answer questions and provide safety information.

There are no developed campgrounds within the monument; backcountry camping is permitted. There are undeveloped campsites along primary roads. No fees or permits for backcountry camping are required. There is a 14-day stay limit. Wilderness skills are essential. Roads to and within the Monument are not paved and may become impassable when wet.

Recommended safety and survival equipment:

- maps of the area
- two full-sized spare tires with jack and lug wrench
- first-aid kit
- basic tool kit
- emergency food and water
- blankets or sleeping bags
- flashlight
- high clearance or four-wheel drive vehicle

Navajo National Monument

PO Box 7717
Shonto, AZ 86045
Phone: 928-672-2700

Navajo National Monument is in northeast Arizona about 140 miles north of Flagstaff. The park preserves three cliff dwellings of the Ancestral Puebloans. Rangers guide visitors on tours of the Keet Seel/ Kawestima and Betatakin/Talastima cliff dwellings. A short half-mile trail from the visitor center leads to an overlook of the Betatakin/Talastima dwelling. There is no entrance fee.

Park Activities
Auto Touring
Biking
Boating
✓ Camping
Climbing
Fishing
✓ Hiking
Horseback Riding
Hunting
Snow Skiing
Swimming
✓ Wildlife Viewing

Information is available from the visitor center located nine miles north of Black Mesa Junction with US 160 on AZ 564. Exhibits feature various artifacts from Anasazi and Navajo culture. A craft shop is also within the visitor center building.

There are two campgrounds within the park. Campsites are available on a first-come, first-served basis; reservations are not accepted. No open-flame fires are allowed; campers must use campstoves or charcoal for cooking.

Canyon View: located near the visitor center, open April through September, 16 sites, no hookups, pit toilets, charcoal grills, no water, no camping fee.

Sunset View: located near the visitor center, open all year, 31 sites, no hookups, one handicap-accessible site, restrooms, drinking water, picnic tables, 28-foot RV length limit, seven day maximum stay, no fee.

Organ Pipe Cactus National Monument

10 Organ Pipe Dr
Ajo, AZ 85321
Phone: 520-387-6849

Organ Pipe Cactus National Monument
is in southern Arizona about 140 miles
south of Phoenix and 22 miles south of
Why. It protects over 330,000 acres of
Sonoran Desert wildlife and landscape.
The monument exhibits an extraordinary
collection of plants, including the organ
pipe cactus, a large cactus rarely found in
the United States. An entrance fee of $8
per vehicle is charged.

Park Activities

✓ Auto Touring
✓ Biking
  Boating
✓ Camping
✓ Climbing
  Fishing
✓ Hiking
✓ Horseback Riding
  Hunting
  Snow Skiing
  Swimming
✓ Wildlife Viewing

Information is available from the Kris
Eggle Visitor Center, located on AZ 85 about 35 miles south of Ajo. The
center is open daily from 8am to 5pm, excluding Thanksgiving Day and
Christmas Day. The visitor center features a museum with photographic
exhibits and dioramas on the Sonoran Desert.

There are two campgrounds within the monument. Campsites in both
are available on a first-come, first-served basis; reservations are not
accepted.

Alamo Canyon: open all year, four sites, $8 per night, no water, pit
toilets, permit required (available at visitor center), 7-day stay limit.
Motorhomes and trailers are not permitted.

Twin Peaks: located along AZ 85, open all year, 208 RV/tent sites,
$12 per night, 40-foot RV length limit, drinking water, restrooms
with showers, picnic tables, grills, dump station, 14-day maximum
stay.

Petrified Forest National Park

PO Box 2217
Petrified Forest, AZ 86028
Phone: 928-524-6228

Petrified Forest National Park is in northeast Arizona. The park features one of the world's largest and most colorful concentrations of petrified wood. Among the park's 93,533 acres are the multi-hued badlands of the Chinle Formation known as the Painted Desert, historic structures, archeological sites, and displays of 225 million-year-old fossils. An entrance fee of $10 is charged.

Park Activities

- ✓ Auto Touring
- ✓ Biking
- Boating
- ✓ Camping
- Climbing
- Fishing
- ✓ Hiking
- ✓ Horseback Riding
- Hunting
- Snow Skiing
- Swimming
- Wildlife Viewing

Information is available from the Painted Desert Visitor Center, which is located near the park's northern entrance off I-40 Exit 311. The visitor center is open all year and provides information, book sales, exhibits, and restrooms. Rainbow Forest Museum, located off US-180 near the park's south entrance, features exhibits of petrified wood, fossils, and displays of prehistoric animals as well as information, book sales, and restrooms.

Backpack camping is allowed within the Petrified Forest National Wilderness Area. A free backcountry permit is required and may be obtained at one of the visitor centers during park hours (7am to 7pm in summer and 8am to 5pm in winter). Backpackers must camp at least one mile away from two designated parking areas.

Saguaro National Park

3693 S Old Spanish Trail
Tucson, AZ 85730
Phone: 520-733-5153 or 520-733-5158

Saguaro National Park is in southern Arizona. It is divided into two districts: Saguaro East (Rincon Mountain District) and Saguaro West (Tucson Mountain District). The park encompasses a total of 91,443 acres. Both districts offer miles of trails for hiking and scenic loop drives. An entrance fee of $10 per vehicle is charged.

Information is available from visitor centers in each district. Both are open daily between 9am and 5pm except Christmas. Both offer slide shows, museums, cactus gardens, and a sales outlet.

Park Activities
✓ Auto Touring
✓ Biking
Boating
✓ Camping
Climbing
Fishing
✓ Hiking
Horseback Riding
Hunting
Snow Skiing
Swimming
✓ Wildlife Viewing

There are no developed campgrounds in either district. Backcountry camping is permitted at six designated campgrounds in the Saguaro Wilderness Area located in Saguaro East. Reservations and a permit is required (fee charged) and can be obtained at the visitor center. Permits are not available after noon on the day of departure. RV campgrounds are available in the surrounding area.

Sunset Crater Volcano National Monument

Flagstaff Area National Monuments
6400 N Hwy 89
Flagstaff, AZ 86004
Phone: 928-526-0502

Sunset Crater Volcano National Monument is in north-central Arizona about 20 miles north of Flagstaff. The main attraction is a large cinder cone rising 1,000 feet above the surrounding landscape. Visitors will also find pueblos and cliff dwellings. The monument is open year-round. An entrance fee of $5 per person is charged.

Park Activities

Auto Touring
Biking
Boating
✓ Camping
Climbing
Fishing
✓ Hiking
Horseback Riding
Hunting
Snow Skiing
Swimming
Wildlife Viewing

Information is available from the visitor center located two miles east of US 89 on Sunset Crater Wupatki Loop Road. The visitor center remains open year-round (closed Christmas Day). Special programs are generally offered during summer months.

There is no camping within the monument. There is, however, one campground managed by the U.S. Forest Service near the visitor center. For more campground information contact the Coconino National Forest at 928-526-0866.

Bonito: located near the visitor center, open early May to early October, 44 sites, no hookups, $18 per night, 42-foot RV length limit, drinking water, flush toilets, reservations not accepted, 14 day stay limit.

Arkansas

1   Buffalo National River
2   Hot Springs National Park

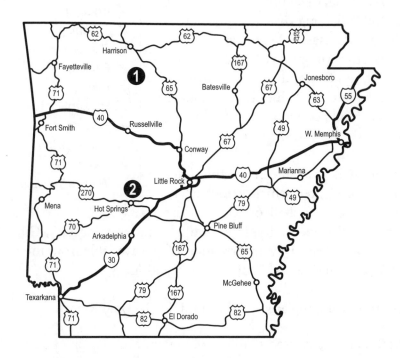

Buffalo National River

402 N Walnut, Suite 136
Harrison, AR 72601
Phone: 870-439-2502

┌─────────────────────────────┐
│ **Park Activities** │

✓	Auto Touring
	Biking
✓	Boating
✓	Camping
	Climbing
✓	Fishing
✓	Hiking
✓	Horseback Riding
✓	Hunting
	Snow Skiing
✓	Swimming
✓	Wildlife Viewing

Buffalo National River preserves 135 miles of the 150-mile long river running across northern Arkansas. It begins as a trickle in the Boston Mountains 15 miles above the park boundary and runs east through the Ozarks into the White River. Massive limestone bluffs contain the free-flowing river. There is no entrance fee.

Information is available from the Tyler Bend Visitor Center, which is located 11 miles north of Marshall on US 65. The visitor center is open all year excluding Thanksgiving Day, Christmas Day, and New Year's Day. Information is also available from the Buffalo Point Ranger Station and Pruitt Ranger Station.

There are 11 camping areas within Buffalo National River.

Buffalo Point: located 17 miles southeast of Yellville on AR 268, open all year, 83 RV/tent sites with water and electric hookups ($17 per night), 20 walk-in tent sites ($12 per night), three sites accessible to the handicapped, 31-foot RV length limit, 14 day maximum stay, picnic tables, fire grates, drinking water, showers, flush toilets, pay phone, dump station, limited facilities in winter. No fees charged mid-November to mid-March. Reservations accepted (877-444-6777).

Carver: located south of Hasty off AR 123, open all year, eight tent sites, $10 per night mid-March to mid-November, picnic tables, vault toilets. No fees charged mid-November to mid-March.

Erbie: located eight miles southwest of Dogpatch via AR 7 and Erbie Campground Road, open all year, 14 drive-in sites and 16 walk-in sites, picnic tables, fire grates, drinking water, flush and vault toilets, pay phone, $10 per night mid-March to mid-November. No fees charged mid-November to mid-March.

Kyles Landing: located about seven miles west of Jasper off AR 74 via Kyles Landing Road, open all year, 33 tent sites, $10 per night mid-March to mid-November, picnic tables, fire grates, drinking water, flush toilets. No fees charged mid-November to mid-March.

Maumee South: located 12 miles northwest of Harriet off AR 27 via CR 52, open all year, primitive campground with open camping, vault toilets, no camping fee.

Ozark: located six miles north of Jasper off AR 7, open all year, 35 tent sites, $10 per night mid-March to mid-November, picnic tables, fire grates, drinking water, flush toilets, pay phone. No fees charged mid-November to mid-March.

Rush: located six miles east of Caney off AR 14 via CR 26, open all year, 12 tent sites, $10 per night mid-March to mid-November, drinking water nearby, fire grates, vault toilets. No fees charged mid-November to mid-March.

Spring Creek: six miles northwest of Harriet via AR 14 and CR 99, open all year, 14 sites, picnic tables, fire grates, vault toilets, no drinking water. No fees charged.

Steel Creek: located four miles northeast of Ponca off AR 74 via Steel Creek Road, open all year, 26 tent sites, $10 per night mid-March to mid-November, picnic tables, fire grates, drinking water nearby, vault toilets, pay phone. Additional horse campground with 14 sites available. No fees charged mid-November to mid-March.

Tyler Bend: located 12 miles northwest of Marshall off US 65 via CR 241 and CR 231, open all year, 28 drive-in sites and 10 walk-in sites, $12 per night mid-March to mid-November, picnic tables, fire grates, drinking water nearby, showers, flush toilets, dump station, pay phone, no hookups, 28-foot RV length limit, 14 day maximum stay. No fees charged mid-November to mid-March.

Woolum: located seven miles southwest of Saint Joe off US 65 via AR 374 and CR 14, open all year, primitive campground with open camping, fire grates, vault toilets, no camping fee, horse campsites available.

Hot Springs National Park

101 Reserve St
Hot Springs, AR 71901
Phone: 501-620-6715

Park Activities
✓ Auto Touring
Biking
Boating
✓ Camping
Climbing
Fishing
✓ Hiking
✓ Horseback Riding
Hunting
Snow Skiing
Swimming
Wildlife Viewing

Hot Springs National Park is in central Arkansas about 50 miles southwest of Little Rock. The park was first established as Hot Springs Reservation on April 20, 1832 to protect hot springs flowing from the southwestern slope of Hot Springs Mountain. The park protects eight historic bathhouses, contains about 5,500 acres and attracts 3.2 million visitors annually.

Information is available from the visitor center located in the former Fordyce Bathhouse on Bathhouse Row in downtown Hot Springs. Bathhouse Row is on Central Avenue (AR Hwy 7) between Reserve and Fountain Streets. The visitor center is open 9am to 5pm year-round except New Year's Day, Thanksgiving Day, and Christmas Day.

There is one campground in the park. It is located on the eastern edge of Hot Springs, just off US 70. Other public campgrounds are nearby.

Gulpha Gorge: open year-round, 43 RV and tent sites, drinking water, picnic tables, restrooms, dump station, pay phone, $10 per night for sites without hookups, $24 per night for sites with full hookups, 14 day maximum stay. Reservations are not accepted; all sites are available on a first-come, first-served basis.

California

1   Channel Islands National Park
2   Death Valley National Park
3   Devil's Postpile National Monument
4   Golden Gate National Recreation Area
5   Joshua Tree National Park
6   Lassen Volcanic National Park
7   Lava Beds National Monument
8   Mojave National Preserve
9   Pinnacles National Monument

10   Point Reyes National Seashore
11   Redwood National and State Parks
12   Santa Monica Mountains
     National Recreation Area
13   Sequoia & Kings Canyon
     National Parks
14   Whiskeytown National
     Recreation Area
15   Yosemite National Park

Channel Islands National Park

1901 Spinnaker Dr
Ventura, CA 93001
Phone: 805-658-5730

Channel Islands National Park consists of five islands in southern California: Anacapa, Santa Cruz, Santa Rosa, San Miguel, and Santa Barbara. The park encompasses 249,354 acres, half of which are under the ocean. Nearly 650,000 visitors come to this park each year. Access is by air or boat. There is no entrance fee.

Park Activities

Auto Touring
Biking
✓ Boating
✓ Camping
Climbing
✓ Fishing
✓ Hiking
Horseback Riding
Hunting
Snow Skiing
✓ Swimming
✓ Wildlife Viewing

Park information is available from the visitor center in Ventura. The visitor center is open between 8:30am and 5pm year-round except on Thanksgiving and Christmas. Visitor contact stations are located on Anacapa Island and Santa Barbara Island.

Camping is available on all five islands. A fee of $15.00 per night is charged at all campgrounds. Reservations are required and can be made by calling 877-444-6777. Campers must be prepared for primitive camping and bring their own supplies including a camp stove, fuel, and water. Supplies and equipment are not available on the islands. Be prepared to carry your camping gear from the landing areas to the campgrounds. All campers must pack out their own trash.

Anacapa Island: open all year, seven campsites with a campground capacity of 30 people, pit toilets, picnic tables. The campground is one-half mile from the dock landing, up 154 steps.

San Miguel Island: open all year, nine campsites with a total capacity of 30 people, pit toilets, picnic tables. The campground is a one-mile hike uphill from the beach landing.

Santa Barbara Island: open all year, ten campsites with a total capacity of 30 people, pit toilets, picnic tables. The campground is one-half mile uphill from the dock landing.

Santa Cruz Island, Scorpion Ranch: open all year, 31 sites with a total capacity of 240 people, pit toilets, picnic tables. Campsites are spread out along the valley floor one-half to one mile up the flats from the beach landing.

Santa Rosa Island: open year-round, 15 campsites with a total capacity of 50 people, pit toilets, picnic tables, running water (most people bring drinking water), shower facilities. Camping on the beach is permitted on a seasonal basis for experienced kayakers and boaters.

Death Valley National Park

PO Box 579
Death Valley, CA 92328
Phone: 760-786-3200

Death Valley National Park in southern
California contains more than 3.3 million
acres of spectacular desert scenery. It
features the lowest point in the western
hemisphere; Badwater is 282 feet below
sea level. More than one million visitors
come to this park each year. An entrance
fee of $20 is charged.

Park Activities
✓ Auto Touring
✓ Biking
Boating
✓ Camping
Climbing
Fishing
✓ Hiking
✓ Horseback Riding
Hunting
Snow Skiing
✓ Swimming
✓ Wildlife Viewing

Information is available from two visitor
centers: Scotty's Castle Visitor Center &
Museum at the north end of the park;
and the Furnance Creek Visitor Center & Museum on CA 190. Both are
open year-round.

There are nine public campgrounds in Death Valley National Park.
Backcountry camping is permitted but your campsite must be two miles
away from any developed area, paved road, or day-use area. Free permits
may be obtained at the visitor center or ranger station.

Emigrant: located along CA 190 about 18 miles east of Panamint
Springs, open all year, ten tent-only sites, water, picnic tables, flush
toilets, no fires allowed, no camping fee, 30 day maximum stay.

Furnace Creek: located along CA 190 about 53 miles east of
Panamint Springs, open all year, reservations accepted (877-444-
6777), 136 RV and tent sites, drinking water, tables, firepits, flush
toilets, dump station, no hookups, $18 per night ($12 mid-April to
mid-October), 14 day maximum stay, 35-foot RV length limit.

Mahogany Flat: located in the Panamint Mountains off Emigrant
Canyon Road, open March to November, accessible to high-
clearance vehicles only (four-wheel drive may be necessary), ten

sites, tables, firepits, pit toilets, no camping fee, no water, 30 day maximum stay.

Mesquite Spring: located three miles south of Scotty's Castle on Grapevine Road, open all year, 30 sites, water, tables, firepits, flush toilets, dump station, $12 per night, 30 day maximum stay, 35-foot RV length limit.

Stovepipe Wells: located in Stovepipe Wells Village along CA 190, open mid-October to mid-April, 190 sites, some tables, some firepits, flush toilets, dump station, water, $12 per night, 30 day maximum stay, 35-foot RV length limit.

Sunset: in Furnace Creek off CA 190, open mid-October to mid-April, 270 RV/tent sites, water, flush toilets, dump station, no fires allowed, $12 per night, 30 day maximum stay, 40-foot RV length limit.

Texas Spring: located one-half mile east of Furnace Creek off CA 190, open mid-October to mid-April, 92 sites, water, tables, firepits, flush toilets, dump station, $14 per night, 30 day maximum stay, 35-foot RV length limit, no generators allowed.

Thorndike: in the Panamint Mountains off Emigrant Canyon Road, open March through November, accessible to high-clearance vehicles only (four-wheel drive may be necessary), six sites, tables, firepits, pit toilets, no camping fee, 30 day maximum stay.

Wildrose: located in the Panamint Mountains off Emigrant Canyon Road, open all year, 23 sites, no camping fee, tables, firepits, pit toilets, 30 day maximum stay. Drinking water is available in spring, summer, and fall. Campground is not accessible to vehicles over 25 feet long.

Devil's Postpile National Monument

PO Box 3999
Mammoth Lakes, CA 93546
Phone: 760-934-2289

Park Activities

Auto Touring
Biking
Boating
✓ Camping
Climbing
✓ Fishing
✓ Hiking
✓ Horseback Riding
Hunting
Snow Skiing
Swimming
✓ Wildlife Viewing

Devil's Postpile National Monument is in central California about 50 miles northwest of Bishop. It contains 800 acres and features the unusual geologic formation known as "the Postpile." Nearly 75 percent of the monument is preserved as part of the Ansel Adams Wilderness. The John Muir and Pacific Crest Trails can be accessed within the monument. Devil's Postpile is open only in summer. Except for vehicles with camping permits, private vehicles are not allowed into the monument; a shuttle bus takes day-use visitors into the monument. An entrance fee of $7 per person is charged. Please note: The U.S. Forest Service, which manages land surrounding the national monument, established this fee in 2002. The fee is required to visit Devil's Postpile National Monument and is not covered by the National Parks Pass.

Information is available from the Devil's Postpile Ranger Station located just inside the monument's entrance. The station is usually open from late June until early October.

There is one National Park Service campground within the monument. A camping permit is required. The U.S. Forest Service manages several campgrounds within a short distance from the monument. All campsites are available on a first-come, first-served basis.

> **Devil's Postpile**: located near the ranger station, open July through September depending on weather, 21 sites, $14 per night, flush toilets, water, 14 day maximum stay. Bear-resistant food boxes are provided.

Golden Gate National Recreation Area

Fort Mason, Building 201
San Francisco, CA 94123
Phone: 415-561-4700

Golden Gate National Recreation Area is in northern California, northwest of San Francisco. It contains over 75,000 acres of land and water, making it one of the largest urban national parks in the world. Approximately 59 miles of bay and ocean shoreline lie within its boundaries. No entrance fee charged.

Information is available from the area's headquarters at Fort Mason, which is at the cross streets of Bay and Franklin in San Francisco. The information center is open all year. Information about all the National Park Service areas in the region can be obtained here. Information is also available from the Alcatraz Island Visitor Center, Marin Headlands Visitor Center, Muir Woods Visitor Center, and the Presidio Visitor Center.

Park Activities
✓ Auto Touring
✓ Biking
✓ Boating
✓ Camping
Climbing
✓ Fishing
✓ Hiking
✓ Horseback Riding
Hunting
Snow Skiing
✓ Swimming
✓ Wildlife Viewing

Golden Gate National Recreation Area offers two hike-in and two walk-in campgrounds. The park does not have accommodations for recreational vehicles. Numerous other campgrounds, both private and public, can be found in the area.

Bicentennial: walk-in campground located near Battery Wallace Picnic Area, open all year, three sites, no fee, portable toilets available, water at the visitor center one mile away, no ground fires, three day maximum stay per year. No pets allowed. Campers may use the BBQ grills in the nearby Battery Wallace Picnic Area.

Hawkcamp: hike-in campground open year-round, three sites, no fee, chemical toilets, picnic tables, no water, campstoves permitted, no ground fires, three day maximum stay per year. No pets allowed.

Haypress: walk-in campground located in the Tennessee Valley in the north end of Marin Highlands, open all year, five sites, no fee, portable restrooms, picnic tables, camp stoves permitted, no ground fires, no water, maximum three day stay per year. No pets allowed.

Kirby Cove: walk-in campground located west of the Golden Gate Bridge, open April through October, four sites, $25 per night, pit toilets, picnic tables, no water, reservations required (877-444-6777), three day maximum stay per year. No pets allowed.

Joshua Tree National Park

74485 National Park Dr
Twentynine Palms, CA 92277
Phone: 760-367-5500

Two deserts come together at Joshua Tree National Park. The Colorado Desert lies within the eastern part of the park and features natural gardens of creosote bush, ocotillo, and cholla cactus. The higher, moister, and slightly cooler Mojave Desert in the western part of the park is where you'll find Joshua trees. An entrance fee of $15 is charged.

Information is available from three visitor centers. The Cottonwood Visitor Center is north of Interstate 10 in the southern part of the park. Joshua Tree Visitor Center is south of CA 62 at the park's western entrance. Oasis Visitor Center is located in Twentynine Palms. All three remain open year-round.

There are eight campgrounds available to visitors within the park.

> **Park Activities**
>
> ✓ Auto Touring
> ✓ Biking
>   Boating
> ✓ Camping
> ✓ Climbing
>   Fishing
> ✓ Hiking
> ✓ Horseback Riding
>   Hunting
>   Snow Skiing
>   Swimming
>   Wildlife Viewing

Belle: located about ten miles south of Twentynine Palms on Utah Trail, open all year, 18 sites, $10 per night, pit toilets, 14 day maximum stay (30 days June through September), no water.

Black Rock: located south of Yucca Valley on Joshua Lane, open all year, reservations accepted (877-444-6777), 100 sites, $15 per night, water and flush toilets available, 14 day maximum stay (30 days June to October), 35-foot RV length limit, nature trails, dump station, horse camp available ($15 per night).

Cottonwood: located on Cottonwood Spring Road about seven miles north of I-10, open year-round, 62 sites, $15 per night, water, flush toilets, dump station, 14 day maximum stay (30 days June through September).

Hidden Valley: 14 miles southeast of Joshua Tree along Park Boulevard, open all year, 39 sites, $10 per night, no water, pit toilets, 14 day maximum stay (30 days June to October), 25-foot RV length limit.

Indian Cove: located about five miles west of Twentynine Palms and three miles south of CA 62 on Indian Cove Road, open all year, reservations accepted (877-444-6777), 101 sites, $15 per night, water available at ranger station, pit toilets, 14 day maximum stay (30 days June through September).

Jumbo Rocks: located 11 miles south of Twentynine Palms along Park Boulevard, open all year, 124 sites, $10 per night, no water, pit toilets, 14 day maximum stay (30 days June through September).

Ryan: 16 miles southeast of Joshua Tree off Park Boulevard, open all year, 31 sites, $10 per night, no water, pit toilets, 14 day maximum stay, horse camp available ($10 per night).

White Tank: 11 miles south of Twentynine Palms, open all year, 15 sites, $10 per night, no water, pit toilets, 14 day maximum stay, 25-foot RV length limit (includes tow vehicle).

Lassen Volcanic National Park

PO Box 100
Mineral, CA 96063
Phone: 530-595-4480

Lassen Volcanic National Park is in northern California, about 50 miles east of Redding. The park contains 106,372 acres and receives around 350,000 visitors each year. All four types of volcanoes in the world can be found in the park. An entrance fee of $10 is charged.

Information is available from the Kohm Yah-mah-nee Visitor Center near the southwest park entrance on CA 89. The visitor center is open daily all year. Information is also available from the Loomis Museum at the norwest park entrance on CA 89. The museum is open late May to late October.

Park Activities
✓ Auto Touring
Biking
✓ Boating
✓ Camping
Climbing
✓ Fishing
✓ Hiking
✓ Horseback Riding
Hunting
✓ Snow Skiing
✓ Swimming
✓ Wildlife Viewing

Lassen Volcanic National Park has eight campgrounds. There are no hookups for recreational vehicles. All campsites have a picnic table, fire ring with grill, and bear-proof storage locker. Backcountry camping is also available; a wilderness permit is required.

Butte Lake: located about 17 miles from Old Station and six miles south of CA 44 via Butte Lake Rd, open June through October (weather permitting), accommodates RVs up to 45 feet long, 101 sites, $16 per night, reservations accepted (877-444-6777), drinking water, flush and vault toilets, boat launch, 14 day maximum stay.

Crags: five miles southeast of Manzanita Lake along CA 89, open mid-June to mid-September, 45 sites, 45-foot RV length limit, $12 per night, drinking water, vault toilets, 14 day maximum stay.

Juniper Lake: located on the east shore of Juniper Lake about 13 miles north of Chester, access road is rough and not recommended for RVs, open late June to mid-October, 18 tent sites, $10 per night, no water, vault toilets, 14 day maximum stay.

Manzanita Lake: located adjacent to and south of Manzanita Lake off CA 89, open late May until snow closure (usually late October), accommodates RVs up to 45 feet long, 179 sites (some pull-thru), $18 per night, reservations accepted (877-444-6777), dump station, drinking water, flush and vault toilets, showers, laundromat, food, gift shop, boat launch, 14 day maximum stay.

Southwest Walk-In: located near the Southwest Entrance Station, open all year, 20 tent sites, drinking water and flush toilets available mid-May through September, $14 per night, 14 day maximum stay. RVs may park overnight in the parking lot (fee applies).

Summit Lake North: located off CA 89 about 12 miles southeast of Manzanita Lake, open late June to mid-September (weather permitting), 46 sites, $18 per night, reservations accepted (877-444-6777), 45-foot RV length limit, drinking water, flush toilets, 7 day maximum stay.

Summit Lake South: located off CA 89 about 12 miles southeast of Manzanita Lake, open late June through October (weather permitting), 48 sites, $16 per night, reservations accepted (877-444-6777), drinking water, vault toilets, 7 day maximum stay.

Warner Valley: located about 17 miles north of Chester via Warner Valley Road (not recommended for RVs), open mid-June through October (weather permitting), 18 sites, $14 per night, drinking water, vault toilets, 14 day maximum stay.

Lava Beds National Monument

PO Box 1240
Tulelake, CA 96134
Phone: 530-667-8113

Lava Beds National Monument is in northeast California about 65 miles west of Alturas. Cinder cones, lava flows, and numerous lava tube caves characterize its 46,500 acres. The park was designated a national monument in 1925. An entrance fee of $10 is charged.

Information is available from the visitor center located near the Indian Well Campground. The center remains open year-round and has a gift shop, natural and cultural history exhibits, and an informative video.

Park Activities

✓ Auto Touring
✓ Biking
   Boating
✓ Camping
   Climbing
   Fishing
✓ Hiking
✓ Horseback Riding
   Hunting
   Snow Skiing
   Swimming
✓ Wildlife Viewing

There is only one campground available to visitors. Campsites are available on a first-come, first-served basis. Sites are suitable for tents, pickup campers, small trailers and motorhomes up to 30 feet. One campsite is accessible to the handicapped.

Indian Well: west of CA 139 via CR 97 and Lava Beds National Monument Road, open all year, 43 sites, $10 per night, drinking water and flush toilets, 14 day maximum stay.

Mojave National Preserve

2701 Barstow Rd
Barstow, CA 92311
Phone: 760-252-6100

Mojave National Preserve is in southeast California. The 1.6-million acre park was established in 1994. The area ranges from creosote bush flats in low areas to pinyon pine and juniper woodlands at higher elevations. The preserve is open year-round. No entrance fee is charged.

Information is available from the park's headquarters in Barstow. A ranger is on duty to help with trip planning. Information is also available at the Hole-in-the-Wall Information Center, located 20 miles north of I-40 via Essex and Black Canyon Roads. The Kelso Depot Visitor Center is about 22 miles north of I-40 via Kelbaker Rd and is open daily (except Christmas Day) from 9am to 5pm.

Park Activities
✓ Auto Touring
✓ Biking
Boating
✓ Camping
✓ Climbing
Fishing
✓ Hiking
✓ Horseback Riding
✓ Hunting
Snow Skiing
Swimming
✓ Wildlife Viewing

There are two developed campgrounds in the preserve. Campsites are available on a first-come, first-served basis. Camping is also available in the Providence Mountains State Recreation Area.

Hole-in-the-Wall: located ten miles north of I-40 via Essex Road and Black Canyon Road, open all year, 35 RV/tent sites, two walk-in tent sites, $12 per night, drinking water, pit toilets, dump station.

Mid Hills: located about 30 miles north of I-40 via Essex Road and Black Canyon Road, open all year, 26 sites, $12 per night, drinking water, pit toilets. The road to the campground is not paved and is not recommended for motorhomes or vehicles pulling trailers.

Pinnacles National Monument

5000 Hwy 146
Paicines, CA 95043
Phone: 831-389-4486

Pinnacles National Monument is located in central California about 30 miles south of Hollister. The 26,425-acre park preserves rocky spires and crags surrounded by rolling hills and mountains. An entrance fee of $5 is charged.

There are two entrances into the park but no through-road. The eastern entrance provides access to most of the park's amenities and facilities, including the campground. The western entrance is primarily used by visitors interested in accessing hiking trails in the Chaparral area. The access road to the western portion of the monument is steep and narrow; RVs are not recommended.

Park Activities
Auto Touring
Biking
Boating
✓ Camping
✓ Climbing
Fishing
✓ Hiking
Horseback Riding
Hunting
Snow Skiing
Swimming
✓ Wildlife Viewing

Information is available from the Bear Gulch Visitor Center located about two miles from the park's eastern entrance.

There is one concession-operated campground in the monument. Food and other supplies are available at the convenience store within the campground. Reservations accepted; call 877-444-6777. Backcountry camping is not permitted.

Pinnacles: located two miles off CA 25 near the park's east entrance, open all year, 36 RV sites with 30-amp electric hookups ($36 per night), 99 tent sites without electricity ($23 per night), restrooms, showers, drinking water, dump station, amphitheater, swimming pool. 831-389-4538

Point Reyes National Seashore

1 Bear Valley Rd
Point Reyes Station, CA 94956
Phone: 415-464-5100

Point Reyes National Seashore is in northern California about 22 miles north of San Francisco. The 65,300-acre area was established in 1962. It remains open all year. There is no entrance fee.

Information is available from three visitor centers. Bear Valley is the park's primary visitor center and is located off Bear Valley Road near Olema; it remains open all year. Information is also available at the Kenneth C. Patrick Visitor Center and the Lighthouse Visitor Center.

Park Activities

Auto Touring
✓ Biking
Boating
✓ Camping
Climbing
Fishing
✓ Hiking
✓ Horseback Riding
Hunting
Snow Skiing
Swimming
✓ Wildlife Viewing

There are four hike-in campgrounds available. Permits are required and are available at the Bear Valley Visitor Center. Camping is limited to a total of four nights. Reservations are required and can be made by calling 877-444-6777.

Coast Camp: open all year, 12 sites, $20 per night, picnic tables, food storage locker, charcoal grills, pit toilets, drinking water.

Glen Camp: open all year, 12 sites, $20 per night, picnic tables, food storage locker, charcoal grills, pit toilets, drinking water.

Sky Camp: open all year, 11 sites, $20 per night, picnic tables, food storage locker, charcoal grills, pit toilets, drinking water.

Wildcat Camp: open all year, 5 sites, $20 per night, picnic tables, food storage locker, charcoal grills, pit toilets, drinking water.

Redwood National and State Parks

1111 Second St
Crescent City, CA 95531
Phone: 707-465-7335

Redwood National and State Parks are located in northwest California. The area is a cooperative management effort between the National Park Service and California Department of Parks and Recreation. Three California state parks and the National Park Service unit make up this area that protects 45 percent of all the old-growth redwood forest remaining in California. There is no entrance fee for the National Park Service unit.

Park Activities

✓ Auto Touring
✓ Biking
✓ Boating
✓ Camping
  Climbing
✓ Fishing
✓ Hiking
✓ Horseback Riding
  Hunting
  Snow Skiing
✓ Swimming
✓ Wildlife Viewing

Information is available from three visitor centers and two information centers. Jedediah Smith Visitor Center is on US 101 at Hiouchi and is open mid-May to mid-September. Prairie Creek Visitor Center is just off US 101 along Newton B. Drury Scenic Parkway and is open all year. The Thomas H. Kuchel Visitor Center is along US 101 at Orick and is open year-round. Crescent City Information Center is at 1111 Second Street in Crescent City and is open daily all year. The Hiouchi Information Center is open dily in summer and is located along US 199 at Hiouchi.

There are four developed campgrounds available to visitors; all are managed by the State of California. Please note that Senior and Access Passes may not be honored at these campgrounds. California does have a similar discount program, however. Other public campgrounds are located within the surrounding national forest.

Elk Prairie: located off US 101 on Newton B. Drury Scenic Parkway in Prairie Creek Redwoods State Park, open all year, 75 RV/tent sites, $35 per night, 27-foot RV length limit (24 feet for trailers),

14 day maximum stay, showers, restrooms, picnic area, trails, fire pits, bearproof lockers, handicap access, no hookups, reservations accepted (800-444-7275).

Gold Bluffs Beach: located in Prairie Creek Redwoods State Park at the end of Davison Road off US 101, open April to September, 26 sites (no hookups), RVs limited to 24 feet long and 8 feet wide, restrooms, solar showers, fire pits, $35 per night, 14 day maximum stay, reservations are not accepted.

Jedediah Smith: located nine miles east of Crescent City along US 199 in Jedediah Smith Redwoods State Park, open all year, 86 RV/tent sites, no hookups, 36-foot RV length limit (31 feet for trailers), restrooms, showers, dump station, bearproof lockers, fire pits, $35 per night, 14 day maximum stay, reservations accepted (800-444-7275).

Mill Creek: located seven miles south of Crescent City off US 101 in Del Norte Coast Redwoods State Park, open May to early September, 145 RV/tent sites (no hookups), $35 per night, 31-foot RV length limit (27 feet for trailers), restrooms, showers, dump station, bearproof lockers, fire pits, handicap access, trails, 14 day maximum stay, reservations accepted (800-444-7275).

Santa Monica Mountains National Recreation Area

401 W Hillcrest Dr
Thousand Oaks, CA 91360
Phone: 805-370-2300

Santa Monica Mountains National Recreation Area is located in southern California, northwest of Los Angeles. The area encompasses 150,000 acres of mountains, canyons, woodlands, and miles of beach. It was established in 1978 and is managed cooperatively by federal, state, and local park agencies. There is no entrance fee.

Information is available from the National Park Service Visitor Center located at 401 West Hillcrest Drive in Thousand Oaks. The center is open daily from 9am to 5pm. Exhibits include interactive displays and historical artwork. Information is also available from the Anthony C. Beilenson Interagency Visitor Center in Calabasas on Mulholland Highway.

Park Activities
✓ Auto Touring
✓ Biking
Boating
✓ Camping
✓ Climbing
✓ Fishing
✓ Hiking
✓ Horseback Riding
Hunting
Snow Skiing
✓ Swimming
✓ Wildlife Viewing

There are four camping areas in the park. All are managed by the State of California. Please note that Senior and Access Passes may not be honored at these areas. California does have a similar discount program, however.

Canyon Family Camp: located in Leo Carrillo State Park west of Malibu along CA 1, open all year, 135 sites, $45 per night, drinking water, flush toilets, showers, dump station, fire rings, seven day stay limit in summer, 31-foot RV length limit, reservations accepted (800-444-7275).

Big Sycamore Canyon Family Camp: located in Point Mugu State Park, open all year, 58 sites, $45 per night, drinking water, flush toilets, showers, dump station, fire rings, reservations accepted (800-444-7275), seven day stay limit in summer, 31-foot RV length limit.

Thornhill Broome Family Camp: located in Point Mugu State Park, open all year, 68 sites, $35 per night, drinking water, chemical toilets, fire rings, seven day stay limit in summer, reservations accepted (800-444-7275).

Malibu Creek Family Camp: located in Malibu Creek State Park, open all year, 62 sites, $45 per night, drinking water, flush toilets, showers, dump station, fire rings, reservations accepted (800-444-7275), seven day maximum stay in summer, 30-foot RV length limit.

Sequoia & Kings Canyon National Parks

47050 Generals Highway
Three Rivers, CA 93271
Phone: 559-565-3341

Sequoia and Kings Canyon National Parks are two separate parks managed as one. Together, the parks preserve immense mountains, deep canyons, and towering sequoia trees. Sequoia National Park contains the highest mountain in the lower 48 states, Mount Whitney. Kings Canyon National Park is home to North America's deepest canyon. An entrance fee of $20 per vehicle is charged.

Park Activities

✓ Auto Touring
  Biking
  Boating
✓ Camping
  Climbing
✓ Fishing
✓ Hiking
✓ Horseback Riding
  Hunting
✓ Snow Skiing
  Swimming
✓ Wildlife Viewing

Park information is available from four visitor centers. Grant Grove Visitor Center in Kings Canyon National Park is three miles east on CA 180 from the Big Stump Entrance Station. Cedar Grove Visitor Center is on CA 180 about 30 miles east of Grant Grove and is only open in summer. The Foothills Visitor Center and Lodgepole Visitor Center are located in Sequoia National Park. The first is on Generals Highway about one mile from the park entrance. The latter is on Lodgepole Road just off Generals Highway about 21 miles from the park entrance.

A total of 14 campgrounds are available. Most have bear-proof food storage that must be used. Reservations are accepted for campsites in Lodgepole and Dorst Creek campgrounds in Sequoia National Park; call 1-877-444-6777. All other campsites are available on a first-come, first-served basis. RVs are not permitted in Atwell Mill, Buckeye Flat, Canyon View, and Cold Spring campgrounds. A limited number of sites can accommodate RVs over 30 feet long. No hookups are available in any of the campgrounds.

Campgrounds in Kings Canyon National Park

Azalea: in the Grant Grove area 3.5 miles from park entrance, open all year, 110 sites, $18 per night, drinking water, tables, fire grills, flush toilets, pay phone, limited RV space, 14 day maximum stay in summer. Near visitor center, market, restaurant, gift shop, and showers.

Canyon View: in Cedar Grove area near Kings River, open as needed from mid-May to early October, 23 sites, $18 per night, flush toilets, pay phone, drinking water, tables, fire grills, 14 day maximum stay in summer. Nearby restaurant, market, showers, laundry, and horseback riding.

Crystal Springs: in the Grant Grove area four miles from the park entrance, open mid-May to mid-September, 36 sites, $18 per night, drinking water, tables, fire grills, flush toilets, pay phone, 14 day maximum stay in summer. Near visitor center, market, post office, gift shop, and restaurant.

Moraine: in the Cedar Grove area down in the canyon along Kings River, open as needed May to October, 120 sites, $18 per night, flush toilets, fire grills, tables, drinking water, 14 day maximum stay in summer. Near restaurant, pay phone, market, showers, laundry, and horseback riding.

Sentinel: in the Cedar Grove area, open May to September, 82 sites, $18 per night, flush toilets, fire grills, tables, drinking water, 14 day maximum stay in summer. Near restaurant, market, pay phone, showers, laundry, and horseback riding.

Sheep Creek: in the Cedar Grove area down in the canyon near Kings River, open May to October, 111 sites, $18 per night, flush toilets, fire grills, tables, drinking water, 14 day maximum stay in summer. Near restaurant, market, pay phone, showers, laundry, and horseback riding.

Sunset: in the Grant Grove area three miles from park entrance, open May to September, 157 sites, $18 per night, drinking water, tables, fire grills, flush toilets, pay phone, 14 day maximum stay in summer. Near visitor center, market, post office, gift shop, showers, and restaurant.

Campgrounds in Sequoia National Park

Atwell Mill: located in the Mineral King area 19 miles from CA 198, open May to October, access road is not recommended for RVs, campground does not accommodate RVs, 21 tent sites, $12 per night, pit toilets, pay phone, fire grills, tables, drinking water, 14 day maximum stay in summer. Near Silver City Resort with restaurant, gifts, limited supplies, and showers.

Buckeye Flat: located off Generals Highway four miles from park entrance and 12 miles from Giant Forest, open March to September, 28 tent sites, $18 per night, flush toilets, fire grills, drinking water, tables, 14 day stay limit in summer.

Cold Springs: located 23 miles from CA 198 up the steep and narrow Mineral King Road, access road not suitable for RVs, campground does not accommodate RVs, open May to October, 39 sites and 9 walk-in sites, $12 per night, pit toilets, pay phone, fire grills, tables, drinking water, 14 day stay limit in summer. Near Silver City Resort (2.5 miles) with restaurant, gifts, limited supplies, and showers.

Dorst Creek: 12 miles north of Giant Forest on Generals Highway, open June to September, reservations accepted (877-444-6777), 218 sites, $20 per night, flush toilets, dump station, pay phone, fire grills, tables, drinking water, 14 day maximum stay.

Lodgepole: located off Generals Highway two miles north of Giant Forest and 21 miles from park entrance, open April to October, reservations accepted (877-444-6777), 214 sites, $18 per night in spring and fall, $20 per night in summer, flush toilets, dump station, pay phone, tables, drinking water, fire grills, 14 day maximum stay in summer. Restaurant, market, gift shop, laundry, and showers nearby.

Potwisha: located four miles from park entrance along CA 198, open all year, 42 sites, $18 per night, flush toilets, dump station, pay phone, fire grills, tables, drinking water, 14 day maximum stay in summer.

South Fork: on South Fork Drive 13 miles southeast of Three Rivers off CA 198, open all year, not recommended for RVs, 10 sites, $12 per night May to October (no fee rest of year), no drinking water, pit toilets, fire grills, tables, 14 day maximum stay in summer.

Whiskeytown National Recreation Area

PO Box 188
Whiskeytown, CA 96095
Phone: 530-246-1225

Whiskeytown National Recreation Area is in northern California, west of Redding. The park was established in 1972 and covers 42,500 acres. Features include mountainous backcountry, a large reservoir, and remains of buildings built during the Gold Rush. The park is accessible year-round. A daily vehicle entrance fee of $5 is charged.

Park Activities

- ✓ Auto Touring
- ✓ Biking
- ✓ Boating
- ✓ Camping
-   Climbing
- ✓ Fishing
- ✓ Hiking
- ✓ Horseback Riding
- ✓ Hunting
-   Snow Skiing
- ✓ Swimming
- ✓ Wildlife Viewing

Information is available from the Whiskeytown Visitor Center located along CA 299 about eight miles west of Redding. The center is open all year. Exhibits depicting the California Gold Rush and a wide selection of books are among the center's features.

There are two developed campgrounds within Whiskeytown National Recreation Area. Numerous primitive tent-only campsites are scattered throughout the area. These are available on a first-come, first-served basis and can only be accessed by traveling on dirt roads; some require the use of four-wheel drive vehicles. Permits are available at the visitor center for $10 per night. Developed campgrounds are listed below.

Brandy Creek: located five miles off CA 299 along Kennedy Drive, open year-round, 37 RV sites, $14 per night in summer, $7 per night the rest of the year, 35-foot RV length limit, 14 day maximum stay, water, dump station, public phone. Sites available on a first-come, first-served basis; reservations are not accepted.

Oak Bottom: concessionaire campground located 13 miles west of Redding on CA 299, open all year, 22 RV sites ($18 per night), 100 tent sites ($20 to $22 per night), reservations accepted during summer season (530-359-2269), restrooms, showers, dump station, phone, 14 day maximum stay mid-May to mid-October (30 days in winter). In winter, sites are available on a first-come, first-served basis only. All sites are $10 per night from mid-October to mid-April. Pets allowed ($2 per night fee). Senior Passes are honored and provide a 50 percent discount off camping fees.

Yosemite National Park

PO Box 577
Yosemite, CA 95389
Phone: 209-372-0200

Yosemite National Park is in central California, about 100 miles east of Modesto. The park encompasses beautiful mountain and valley scenery in the Sierra Nevada Mountains. An entrance fee of $20 per vehicle is charged. The park remains open year-round but some roads may close due to snow.

Visitor centers are located in Yosemite Valley (open year-round) and Tuolumne Meadows (summer only). Information stations are located in Wawona and Big Oak Flat. Both are open spring through fall.

Park Activities

- ✓ Auto Touring
- ✓ Biking
- ✓ Boating
- ✓ Camping
- ✓ Climbing
- ✓ Fishing
- ✓ Hiking
- ✓ Horseback Riding
-   Hunting
- ✓ Snow Skiing
- ✓ Swimming
- ✓ Wildlife Viewing

There are 13 campgrounds in Yosemite National Park. Backcountry camping is allowed but a permit is required (available free from the visitor centers). Camping is also available in national forest land surrounding the park.

Bridalveil Creek: 27 miles from Yosemite Valley off Glacier Point Road, open July to September, sites available on a first-come first-served basis, 14 day maximum stay, 35-foot RV length limit (24 feet for trailers), 110 sites, $14 per night, water, flush toilets, no hookups.

Camp 4: walk-in campsites in the Yosemite Valley area, open year-round, 35 sites available on a first-come first-served basis, $5 per person, drinking water, flush toilets. Sites are rented on a per person basis and up to six people will be placed in each campsite regardless of the number of people in your party. Pets not allowed.

Crane Flat: on Big Oak Flat Road (CA 120) 17 miles west of Yosemite Valley, open June to October, reservations required (877-444-6777), 166 sites, $20 per night, water, flush toilets, 14 day maximum stay, 40-foot RV length limit (30 feet for trailers), no hookups.

Hodgdon Meadow: on Big Oak Flat Road (CA 120) 25 miles west of Yosemite Valley, open year-round, reservations required in summer (877-444-6777), 105 sites, $20 per night mid-April to mid-October, $14 per night rest of year, drinking water, flush toilets, 14 day maximum stay, 40-foot RV length limit (30 feet for trailers), no hookups.

Lower Pines: in the Yosemite Valley area, open March to October, reservations required (877-444-6777), seven day maximum stay in summer, 60 sites, $20 per night, water, flush toilets, dump station nearby, showers and laundry nearby, 40-foot RV length limit (35 feet for trailers), no hookups.

North Pines: in the Yosemite Valley area, open April to November, reservations required (877-444-6777), seven day maximum stay in summer, 81 sites, $20 per night, water, flush toilets, dump station nearby, shower and laundry facilities nearby, 40-foot RV length limit (35 feet for trailers), no hookups.

Porcupine Flat: on Tioga Pass Road about 30 miles east of Big Oak Flat Entrance, open July to October, 52 sites, $10 per night, pit toilets, 14 day maximum stay, 24-foot RV length limit (20 feet for trailers), no hookups, no water. Pets not allowed. Reservations not accepted.

Tamarack Flat: about 15 miles east of Big Oak Flat Entrance off Tioga Pass Road, open June to October, 52 sites, $10 per night, 14 day maximum stay, pit toilets, no water, no hookups. Reservations are not accepted. Three-mile access road is not suitable for trailers or large RVs, inquire at visitor center. Pets not allowed.

Tuolumne Meadows: along CA 120 (Tioga Pass Road) about six miles west of Tioga Pass Entrance, open July to September, 304 sites, reservations accepted (877-444-6777), water, flush toilets, dump station nearby, $20 per night, 14 day maximum stay, 35-foot RV length limit, no hookups, showers nearby.

Upper Pines: in the Yosemite Valley area, open year-round, reservations required in summer (877-444-6777), seven day maximum stay in summer, 238 sites, $20 per night, water, flush toilets, dump station, showers and laundry nearby, 35-foot RV length limit (24 feet for trailers), no hookups.

Wawona: off CA 41 about eight miles north of Fish Camp, open all year, seven day maximum stay in summer, 93 RV/tent sites, $20 per night ($14 Oct-Apr), water, flush toilets, reservations required in summer (877-444-6777), 35-foot RV length limit, no hookups, dump station nearby.

White Wolf: one mile north of Tioga Pass Road about 22 miles east of Big Oak Flat Entrance, open July to September, 74 sites, $14 per night, drinking water, flush toilets, 14 day maximum stay, 27-foot RV length limit (24 feet for trailers), no hookups. Reservations are not accepted.

Yosemite Creek: south of Tioga Pass Road about 30 miles east of Big Oak Flat Entrance, open July to September, 75 sites, $10 per night, pit toilets, 14 day maximum stay, no drinking water and no hookups. Five-mile access road not suitable for RVs. Reservations not accepted.

Colorado

1   Black Canyon of the Gunnison National Park
2   Colorado National Monument
3   Curecanti National Recreation Area
4   Dinosaur National Monument
5   Great Sand Dunes National Park & Preserve
6   Mesa Verde National Park
7   Rocky Mountain National Park

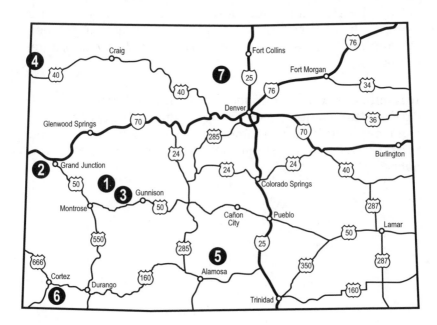

Black Canyon of the Gunnison National Park

102 Elk Creek
Gunnison, CO 81230
Phone: 970-641-2337

Black Canyon of the Gunnison National Park is in western Colorado about 75 miles southeast of Grand Junction. It features narrow canyon walls that drop almost vertically over 2,000 feet to the Gunnison River. Numerous scenic overlooks are easily accessed by car or a short walk. An entrance fee of $15 is charged.

Information is available from the visitor center located on South Rim Drive about two miles from the south rim entrance. Features include exhibits and orientation programs. The visitor center remains open all year.

Park Activities

- ✓ Auto Touring
- Biking
- Boating
- ✓ Camping
- ✓ Climbing
- ✓ Fishing
- ✓ Hiking
- ✓ Horseback Riding
- Hunting
- Snow Skiing
- Swimming
- ✓ Wildlife Viewing

There are two campgrounds within the park. Reservations may be made for South Rim Campground Loops A and B only (877-444-6777).

North Rim: located 11 miles south of Crawford on Black Canyon Road, open spring to fall, 13 sites, $12 per night, pit toilets, tables, grills, water in summer, no hookups, 14 day maximum stay, 35-foot RV length limit.

South Rim: located 15 miles east of Montrose via CO 347, Loop A is open year-round; Loops B & C are open spring to fall, 88 sites, $12 per night, electric hookups available in Loop B only ($18 per night), pit toilets, tables, grills, water available in summer, 14 day maximum stay, 35-foot RV length limit.

Colorado National Monument

1750 Rim Rock Dr
Fruita, CO 81521
Phone: 970-858-3617 ext 360

Colorado National Monument is in west-central Colorado about 12 miles west of Grand Junction. It was established in 1911 and contains about 20,500 acres. Features include sheer-walled canyons, soaring arches, unusual formations, dinosaur fossils, and remains of prehistoric Indian cultures. The park is open all year. An entrance fee of $10 per vehicle is charged.

Park Activities
✓ Auto Touring
✓ Biking
Boating
✓ Camping
✓ Climbing
Fishing
✓ Hiking
✓ Horseback Riding
Hunting
Snow Skiing
Swimming
✓ Wildlife Viewing

Maps and brochures are available from the visitor center located four miles inside the park from the west entrance. The visitor center is open daily except December 25th. Features include an audiovisual program, exhibits, and a bookstore.

There is one campground within the monument. Wood campfires are prohibited. A maximum of seven people per site is allowed. All campsites are available on a first-come, first-served basis. Backcountry camping is permitted; a permit is required and is available for free at the visitor center.

Saddlehorn: located along the park road about four miles from the west entrance, open all year, 80 sites, some pull-through, $20 per night, flush toilets, drinking water, charcoal grills, picnic tables, no water in winter, 40-foot RV length limit, 14 day maximum stay. Pets are allowed.

Curecanti National Recreation Area

102 Elk Creek
Gunnison, CO 81230
Phone: 970-641-2337

Curecanti National Recreation Area is in
west-central Colorado between Montrose
and Gunnison. Three lakes extend 40
miles along the Gunnison River and
the Black Canyon to form the heart of
this recreation area. It was established
in 1965 and encompasses nearly 42,000
acres. There is no entrance fee except at
East Portal, which is $15 per vehicle (the
entrance fee to the Black Canyon of the
Gunnison National Park).

Park Activities

✓ Auto Touring
  Biking
✓ Boating
✓ Camping
✓ Climbing
✓ Fishing
✓ Hiking
✓ Horseback Riding
✓ Hunting
  Snow Skiing
✓ Swimming
✓ Wildlife Viewing

There are two visitor centers: Cimarron and Elk Creek. The Cimarron
Visitor Center (open in summer) is located near the town of Cimarron,
Colorado, 35 miles west of Gunnison on US 50. Elk Creek is 16 miles
west of Gunnison on US 50 and is open year-round.

There are nine campgrounds in the park. Reservable sites are available in
Elk Creek, Lake Fork, and Stevens Creek Campgrounds. Several boat-in
campsites are scattered along the lakes.

Cimarron: located 20 miles east of Montrose on US 50, open
spring to fall, 21 sites (5 pull-thru), $12 per night, picnic tables, fire
grills, water, flush toilets, dump station.

Dry Gulch: located just north of US 50 about 17 miles west of
Gunnison, open spring to fall, nine sites, $12 per night, picnic
tables, fire grates, vault toilets, water, horse corral.

East Portal: 18 miles east of Montrose via US 50, CO 347 and East
Portal Road, open spring to fall, 15 sites, $12 per night, picnic
tables, fire grates, vault toilets, water. Vehicles exceeding 22 feet

in length (including trailer) are not permitted on the East Portal Road because of the steep 16% grade and sharp, narrow curves. Campground is accessed by traveling through Black Canyon of the Gunnison National Park, which charges an entrance fee.

Elk Creek: 16 miles west of Gunnison on US 50, open all year, 160 sites (includes 20 pull-thru sites and 16 walk-in sites), $12 per night (sites with electric hookups available in Loop D for $18 per night), some reservable sites (877-444-6777), water, showers, flush and vault toilets, dump station, marina, boat ramp, restaurant (summer only), 14 day maximum stay.

Gateview: located at the extreme south end of the Lake Fork Arm of Blue Mesa Reservoir, open spring to fall, six sites, no fee, picnic tables, fire grates, vault toilets, water. Access the campground from US 50 by traveling southwest on CO 149 about 25 miles and then north 6 miles on the gravel Blue Mesa Cutoff Road.

Lake Fork: 27 miles west of Gunnison off US 50 on CO 92, open late spring to fall, 90 sites, $12 per night, some reservable sites (877-444-6777), water, flush and vault toilets, showers (summer only), marina, boat ramp, dump station, picnic tables, fire grills.

Ponderosa: located at the northwest end of the Soap Creek Arm of Blue Mesa Reservoir, open spring to fall, 28 sites, $12 per night, picnic tables, fire grates, vault toilets, water, horse corral. Campground is seven miles north of US 50 on the gravel Soap Creek Road, which can become muddy and hazardous or impassable when wet.

Red Creek: located just north of US 50 about 19 miles west of Gunnison, open spring to fall, one individual sites and one group site, $12 per night ($28 for group site), picnic tables, fire grates, vault toilets, water.

Stevens Creek: 12 miles west of Gunnison along US 50, open late May to fall, 53 sites, $12 per night, some reservable sites (877-444-6777), water, vault toilets, boat ramp, 14 day maximum stay.

Dinosaur National Monument

4545 E Highway 40
Dinosaur, CO 81610
Phone: 970-374-3000

Dinosaur National Monument is in northwest Colorado about 110 miles north of Grand Junction. Part of the monument is in northeastern Utah. The monument was established in 1915 and encompasses over 210,000 acres. Features include deep, narrow gorges, sandstone cliffs along the Green and Yampa Rivers, and one of the world's largest concentrations of fossilized dinosaur bones. The monument remains open year-round unless closed by adverse weather. An entrance fee of $10 is charged only in the Dinosaur Quarry area in Utah.

Park Activities

✓ Auto Touring
✓ Biking
  Boating
✓ Camping
✓ Climbing
✓ Fishing
✓ Hiking
  Horseback Riding
  Hunting
  Snow Skiing
  Swimming
✓ Wildlife Viewing

Information is available from the Canyon Area Visitor Center (park headquarters) located two miles east of Dinosaur, Colorado, on US Highway 40. Exhibits and a ten-minute orientation program provide information about the monument's scenic canyon country. Information is also available from the Quarry Visitor Center, which is located seven miles north of Jensen, Utah, off Highway 149.

There are six developed campgrounds within the monument. Campsites are available on a first-come, first-served basis; reservations are not accepted. Most of the campgrounds do not fill up except on Labor Day and Memorial Day. Backcountry camping is allowed; a free permit is required.

> **Deerlodge**: located 53 miles east of the Canyon Area Visitor Center at the extreme eastern end of the monument, open all year, seven tent sites, $8 per night, water, vault toilets, picnic tables, fire pits, 14 day maximum stay. When water is shut off for the winter season, there is no charge for camping.

Echo Park: located 38 miles north of the Canyon Area Visitor Center at the end of Echo Park Road, open all year, 22 sites, $8 per night in summer (free in fall, winter, and spring), water, vault toilets, 14 day maximum stay. Access is dependent on weather; the last 13 miles of road are unpaved and impassable when wet. The road also requires a high-clearance vehicle.

Gates of Lodore: located about 50 miles northwest of Maybell off CO 318, open all year, 17 sites, $8 per night, water, vault toilets, picnic tables, fire pits, 14 day maximum stay, 35-foot RV length limit. When water is shut off for the winter season, there is no charge for camping.

Green River: located three miles east of the Quarry Visitor Center, open April to October, 80 sites, $12 per night, drinking water, restrooms, picnic tables, fire pits, 14 day maximum stay, 35-foot RV length limit.

Rainbow Park: located 24 miles northeast of Jensen, Utah, off Island Park Road, open all year, three tent sites, no camping fee, vault toilet, picnic tables, fire pits, no water, 14 day maximum stay. To reach the campground from Jensen, follow UT 149 to Brush Creek Road to Island Park Road. Some roads become impassable when wet.

Split Mountain: located two miles east of the Quarry Visitor Center, open all year, four tent sites, no fee, drinking water, vault toilets, picnic tables, fire pits, 14 day maximum stay. In summer, the campground is used only for group camping. Water is not available in winter.

Great Sand Dunes National Park & Preserve

11999 Highway 150
Mosca, CO 81146
Phone: 719-378-6399

Great Sand Dunes National Park and Preserve is in southern Colorado about 120 miles southwest of Pueblo. The 149,500-acre park features some of the tallest sand dunes in North America. The park is open year-round. A $3 entrance fee is charged.

Information is available from the visitor center located along CO 150. It remains open all year. Features include a 20-minute video, exhibits, and bookstore.

Park Activities

✓ Auto Touring
  Biking
  Boating
✓ Camping
✓ Climbing
✓ Fishing
✓ Hiking
✓ Horseback Riding
  Hunting
  Snow Skiing
  Swimming
✓ Wildlife Viewing

There is one developed campground within the park. Half of the park's camspites are reservable by calling 877-444-6777. Backcountry camping is permitted at designated sites, in the dune wilderness, and in the national preserve; a free permit is required.

Pinyon Flats: located one mile north of the visitor center, open all year, 88 RV/tent sites, $20 per night, fire grates, picnic tables, flush toilets, dump station, drinking water (April to October), 14 day maximum stay, 35-foot RV length limit. Pets are allowed in the campground.

Mesa Verde National Park

PO Box 8
Mesa Verde, CO 81330
Phone: 970-529-4465

Mesa Verde National Park is in southwest Colorado about 40 miles west of Durango. Features of the park include Ancestral Puebloan structures and cliff dwellings dating from 550 A.D. to 1300 A.D. An entrance fee of $15 is charged in summer ($10 spring and fall).

Information is available from the Far View Visitor Center located 15 miles from the park entrance. The visitor center is open April to October. Features include exhibits of historic Native American jewelry, pottery, and baskets. Tickets for cliff dwelling tours must be purchased here.

There is one concession-operated campground within the park. Campsite reservations can be made by calling 1-800-449-2288.

> **Morefield**: located four miles from the park entrance, open May to October, 267 sites (15 full hookup sites, reservations required), rates start at $26 per night, picnic tables, grills, drinking water, showers, flush toilets, dump station, laundry, gas station, general store, 14 day maximum stay.

Park Activities

Auto Touring
Biking
Boating
✓ Camping
Climbing
Fishing
✓ Hiking
Horseback Riding
Hunting
Snow Skiing
Swimming
✓ Wildlife Viewing

Rocky Mountain National Park

1000 Highway 36
Estes Park, CO 80517
Phone: 970-586-1206

Rocky Mountain National Park is
in north-central Colorado about 70
miles northwest of Denver. The park
encompasses over 265,000 acres of some
of the most beautiful mountain scenery
in Colorado. Trail Ridge Road, an All-
American Road Scenic Byway, crosses
the park and the Continental Divide.
The road provides views of numerous
mountain peaks stretching above 14,000
feet. An entrance fee of $20 is charged.

Park Activities

- ✓ Auto Touring
- ✓ Biking
- Boating
- ✓ Camping
- ✓ Climbing
- ✓ Fishing
- ✓ Hiking
- ✓ Horseback Riding
- Hunting
- ✓ Snow Skiing
- Swimming
- ✓ Wildlife Viewing

Information is available from several visitor centers within the park.
The Alpine Visitor Center is located at Fall River Pass at the junction of
Trail Ridge and Old Fall River roads, four miles east of the Continental
Divide. Beaver Meadows is open year-round and is on US Hwy 36, three
miles west of Estes Park. Fall River is on US Hwy 34, five miles west of
Estes Park, at the Fall River entrance to the park. Kawuneeche is one
mile north of Grand Lake on US 34 near the park's western entrance.
Moraine Park Visitor Center is on Bear Lake Road about 1.5 miles from
the Beaver Meadows Entrance.

There are five campgrounds within Rocky Mountain National Park.
Reservations are accepted for sites in Aspenglen, Glacier Basin, and
Moraine Park; call 877-444-6777. No hookups or showers are available
in any of the campgrounds.

Aspenglen: located just inside the Fall River entrance on US 34
five miles west of Estes Park, open May to September, 54 sites, $20
per night, 7 day stay limit, hiking trails, 30-foot RV length limit.
Reservations recommended. Pets allowed.

Glacier Basin: located seven miles west of Beaver Meadows Visitor Center on Bear Lake Road, open June to early September, 150 sites, $20 per night, 7 day maximum stay, 35-foot RV length limit, flush toilets, dump station, phones. Pets allowed.

Longs Peak: located just off CO 7 nine miles south of Estes Park, open all year, 26 tent-only sites, $20 per night in summer ($14 per night when water is shut off), drinking water in summer, 7 day maximum stay in summer (14 days rest of year). Pets allowed.

Moraine Park: seven miles west of Estes Park off Bear Lake Road, open all year, 245 sites, $20 per night in summer ($14 per night when water is unavailable), 40-foot RV length limit, 7 day maximum stay in summer (14 days rest of year), flush toilets, dump station, horseback riding nearby, hiking trails. Reservations recommended. Pets allowed.

Timber Creek: located ten miles north of Grand Lake on US 34, open all year, 98 sites, $20 per night in summer, $14 per night when water is unavailable, flush toilets, dump station, 30-foot RV length limit, 7 day maximum stay in summer (14 days rest of year). Pets allowed.

Florida

1   Big Cypress National Preserve
2   Biscayne National Park
3   Canaveral National Seashore
4   Dry Tortugas National Park
5   Everglades National Park
6   Gulf Islands National Seashore

Big Cypress National Preserve

33100 Tamiami Trail E
Ochopee, FL 34141
Phone: 239-695-1201

Big Cypress National Preserve is in southern Florida between Miami and Naples. The 729,000-acre area was set aside in 1974 to protect the Big Cypress Watershed. There is no entrance fee.

Information is available from the Oasis Visitor Center on US 41 (Tamiami Trail), half-way between Naples and Miami. Features include a 15-minute movie about the preserve, a wildlife exhibit, and book sales. Information is also available from the Big Cypress Swamp Welcome Center, which is on US-41 about 35 miles east of Naples, Florida.

Park Activities
✓ Auto Touring
✓ Biking
Boating
✓ Camping
Climbing
✓ Fishing
✓ Hiking
Horseback Riding
✓ Hunting
Snow Skiing
Swimming
✓ Wildlife Viewing

There are six campgrounds within Big Cypress National Preserve. Campsites are available on a first-come, first served basis; reservations are not accepted. Camping is limited to 10 days.

Bear Island: primitive campground about 20 miles north of US 41 (Tamiami Trail) via CR 839, open all year, 40 sites, no camping fee, no water or restrooms.

Burns Lake: primitive campground just north of US 41 (Tamiami Trail) about five miles east of Ochopee, open August to January, 14 sites, no camping fee, no water. Vault toilets located near day-use area.

Midway: east of Monroe Station on US 41, open all year, 26 RV sites with hookups ($19 per night), 10 tent sites ($16 per night), drinking water, restrooms, dump station.

Mitchell's Landing: primitive campground west of Fortymile Bend on CR 94, open all year, 15 sites, no camping fee, no water or restrooms.

Monument Lake: near Monroe Station on US 41, 26 RV sites, 10 tent sites, $16 per night, open August to April, flush toilets, drinking water, cold showers, no hookups. Camping fees charged December to April, otherwise free.

Pinecrest: primitive campground west of Fortymile Bend on CR 94, open all year, 10 sites, no camping fee, no water, no restrooms.

Biscayne National Park

9700 SW 328th St
Homestead, FL 33033
Phone: 305-230-7275

Biscayne National Park is in southern
Florida, south of Miami. Ninety-five
percent of the park is covered by water. A
park concessionaire offers several ways to
explore the park with glass bottom boat
tours, snorkeling trips, dive trips, island
excursions, and canoe or kayak rentals.

Park information is available from the
Dante Fascell Visitor Center, located nine
miles east of Homestead on SW 328th
Street. Features include films, art gallery,
interpretive programs, a bookstore, picnic area, restrooms, and a short
walking trail.

Park Activities

Auto Touring
Biking
✓ Boating
✓ Camping
Climbing
✓ Fishing
✓ Hiking
Horseback Riding
Hunting
Snow Skiing
✓ Swimming
✓ Wildlife Viewing

There are two campgrounds for tent-only camping within the park.
Campsites are available on a first-come, first-served basis; no reservations
are accepted. Access to either campground is by boat only. To arrange for
transportation, call the park's concessionaire at 305-230-1100.

Boca Chita Key: open all year, picnic tables, grills, saltwater toilets,
no fresh water, 14 day maximum stay, $15 per night, $20 per night
if you have a boat in the harbor.

Elliott Key: open all year, picnic tables, grills, restrooms, drinking
water, cold water showers, trails, 14 day maximum stay, 40 sites,
$15 per night, $20 per night if you have a boat in the harbor.

Canaveral National Seashore

212 S Washington Ave
Titusville, FL 32796
Phone: 321-267-1110

Canaveral National Seashore is situated on a barrier island in east-central Florida near Titusville. The 57,600-acre area preserves the natural beach, dune, marsh, and lagoon habitats for many species of birds. Kennedy Space Center occupies the southern end of the island. Temporary closure is possible due to launch-related activities. An entrance fee of $5 per car, per day is charged.

Park Activities

Auto Touring
✓ Biking
✓ Boating
✓ Camping
Climbing
✓ Fishing
✓ Hiking
✓ Horseback Riding
✓ Hunting
Snow Skiing
✓ Swimming
✓ Wildlife Viewing

The Apollo Visitor Center, located at 7611 S Atlantic Ave in New Smyrna Beach, Florida, is currently closed due to structural damage. A temporary facility is located next to the original site for obtaining information.

There are no developed campgrounds in Canaveral National Seashore. Island camping is permitted year-round on several islands in Mosquito Lagoon. Boats or canoes are required to get to these sites. No facilities are available. A camping permit is required; the cost is $10 per night for one to six people and $20 per night for groups of seven or more. Permits are available at the information center. Reservations may be made by phone or in person up to seven days in advance.

Dry Tortugas National Park

PO Box 6208
Key West, FL 33041
Phone: 305-242-7700

Dry Tortugas National Park lies about 70 miles west of Key West. The area is known for its bird and marine life, and its legends of pirates and sunken gold. Fort Jefferson, the largest of the 19th century American coastal forts, is a central feature. The park is open all year and can only be reached by boat or plane. A $5 entrance fee is charged.

Information is available from the visitor center located inside Fort Jefferson on Garden Key. It has exhibits on the history of Fort Jefferson and a video describing the park's history and natural resources. The visitor center remains open year-round.

There is one primitive campground in Dry Tortugas National Park. Campers must bring all supplies including fresh water, fuel, ice, and food. All sites are available on a first-come, first-served basis; no reservations accepted. All trash must be carried out upon departure.

> **Garden Key**: open all year, located south of Fort Jefferson a short walk from the public dock, 10 sites, 8 individual sites can accommodate up to six people and three tents, $3 per person per night, picnic tables, grills, composting toilets. Vessels may anchor between sunset and sunrise in a designated anchorage area.

Park Activities

Auto Touring
Biking
✓ Boating
✓ Camping
Climbing
✓ Fishing
Hiking
Horseback Riding
Hunting
Snow Skiing
✓ Swimming
Wildlife Viewing

Everglades National Park

40001 State Road 9336
Homestead, FL 33034
Phone: 305-242-7700

Everglades National Park is in southern Florida about 50 miles southwest of Miami. It is the only subtropical preserve in North America. Ranger led walks and talks are offered year-round. Boat tours are also available. An entrance fee of $10 is charged.

Information is available at four visitor centers. The Ernest F. Coe Visitor Center (open year-round) is located at the main park entrance west of Homestead and Florida City. It features educational displays, orientation films, and brochures. The Flamingo Visitor Center is 38 miles southwest of the main entrance at the southern end of the park. It is open during winter and intermittently during summer. The Gulf Coast Visitor Center (open all year) is located 5 miles south of US 41 (Tamiami Trail) on FL 29 in Everglades City. Shark Valley Visitor Center is located along US 41 about 70 miles east of Naples or 25 miles west of Florida Turnpike Exit 25.

Park Activities
Auto Touring
✓ Biking
✓ Boating
✓ Camping
Climbing
✓ Fishing
✓ Hiking
Horseback Riding
Hunting
Snow Skiing
Swimming
✓ Wildlife Viewing

There are two developed campgrounds within the park. Nearly 50 primitive camping areas are scattered throughout the park. Permits are required for backcountry camping ($10 for the permit and $2 per person, per night).

Flamingo: located at the end of the main park road in Flamingo, open all year, reservations accepted (877-444-6777), 234 drive-in sites (41 with electric hookups, $30 per night) and 40 walk-in sites, $16 per night, cold showers, two dump stations, picnic tables, grills, amphitheater, public telephone, 14 day maximum stay November through March.

Long Pine Key: located seven miles from main entrance, open all year, 108 RV/tent sites, no hookups, $16 per night, 36-foot RV length limit, restrooms, drinking water, public phones, dump station, picnic area, amphitheater, hiking trails. Sites available on a first-come, first-served basis; reservations not accepted.

Gulf Islands National Seashore

1801 Gulf Breeze Parkway
Gulf Breeze, FL 32563
Phone: 850-934-2600 or 228-875-9057

Gulf Islands National Seashore consists of 12 separate units stretching 160 miles from Cat Island, Mississippi, to the eastern tip of Santa Rosa Island in Florida. The 135,607-acre park was established in 1971. Features include white sand beaches, historic forts, and nature trails. An entrance fee of $8 per vehicle is charged.

Park Activities
Auto Touring
✓ Biking
✓ Boating
✓ Camping
Climbing
✓ Fishing
✓ Hiking
✓ Horseback Riding
✓ Hunting
Snow Skiing
✓ Swimming
✓ Wildlife Viewing

Information is available from four visitor centers. Fort Barrancas is in Pensacola Naval Air Station, Florida. The park's headquarters can be found in Gulf Breeze at Naval Live Oaks. William M. Colmer Visitor Center is located in Ocean Springs, Mississippi. Fort Pickens is located approximately 16 miles southwest of Pensacola. All of the visitor centers are open year-round except on Christmas Day.

There are two developed campgrounds available to visitors. Primitive camping is allowed on the eastern end of Perdido Key and on Horn, Petit Bois, and East Ship Islands.

Davis Bayou: located in Ocean Springs, Mississippi two miles south of US 90, open all year, 51 RV/tent sites, $16 per night, all sites have electric and water hookups, hot showers, amphitheater, playground, nature trails, public phone, flush toilets, dump station, 14 day maximum stay, 45-foot RV length limit. Campsites available on a first-come, first-served basis; reservations not accepted.

Fort Pickens: located on the west end of Santa Rosa Island about nine miles west of Gulf Breeze, open all year, 180 sites with electric and water hookups, $20 per night, flush toilets, showers, drinking water, dump station, 14 day maximum stay. Reservations accepted (877-444-6777).

Georgia

1   Cumberland Island National Seashore

Cumberland Island National Seashore

101 Wheeler St
Saint Marys, GA 31558
Phone: 912-882-4336

Cumberland Island National Seashore is in southeast Georgia, seven miles east of Saint Marys. It was established in 1972 and encompasses 36,415 acres of land and water. The island is accessible by a concession-operated passenger ferry. A fee of $4 per person per visit is charged in addition to ferry prices.

Visitors may obtain information from the Mainland Visitor Information Center in Saint Marys. It remains open all year, except Christmas Day. A nearby museum contains a collection of artifacts from Cumberland Island.

Park Activities

Auto Touring
✓ Biking
✓ Boating
✓ Camping
Climbing
✓ Fishing
✓ Hiking
Horseback Riding
Hunting
Snow Skiing
Swimming
✓ Wildlife Viewing

All camping on Cumberland Island is limited to seven days. Backcountry campsites range from 5.5 to 10.5 miles from the ferry dock. Reservations are recommended and may be made up to six months in advance.

Backcountry: open all year, no facilities, $2 per person per night, drinking water should be treated, campfires not permitted; portable stoves suggested.

Sea Camp: open all year, 16 individual sites, $4 per person per night, restrooms, cold showers, drinking water, grills, fire rings, picnic tables.

Stafford: open all year, $2 per person per night, restrooms, showers, fire rings, drinking water should be treated. Sites are assigned at the Sea Camp Ranger Station.

Hawaii

1   Haleakala National Park
2   Hawaii Volcanoes National Park

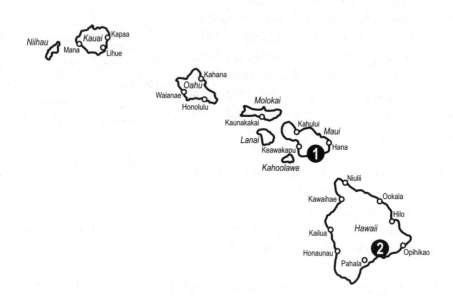

Haleakala National Park

PO Box 369
Makawao, HI 96768
Phone: 808-572-4400

Haleakala National Park preserves the volcanic landscape of the upper slopes of Haleakala on the island of Maui. The park was established in 1916 and preserves over 30,000 acres. The northern entrance is reached from Pukalani by following HI 377 and HI 378. Eastern access is via HI 31 from Hana. An entrance fee of $10 per vehicle is charged.

> ## Park Activities
>
> Auto Touring
> Biking
> Boating
> ✓ Camping
> Climbing
> Fishing
> ✓ Hiking
> ✓ Horseback Riding
> Hunting
> Snow Skiing
> ✓ Swimming
> ✓ Wildlife Viewing

Information is available from the park headquarters located one mile from the park's northern entrance. Information may also be obtained from the Haleakala Visitor Center, near the summit of Haleakala. At the park's east entrance is the Kipahulu Visitor Center.

There are two vehicle-accessible campgrounds and two that are accessed only by hiking to them. Only pit toilets are provided at the hike-in campgrounds. Both require a free backcountry permit, which is available at park headquarters. Three wilderness cabins are also available; contact the park for more information.

Hosmer Grove: located near the park's northern entrance, open all year, picnic tables, grills, drinking water, pit toilets, three day maximum stay. Campsites are available on a first-come, first-served basis. A self-guided nature trail begins and ends at the campground.

Kipahulu: located near the ocean at the park's east entrance, open all year, picnic tables, grills, pit toilets, three day maximum stay. Sites available on a first-come, first-served basis. No drinking water, you must bring your own.

Hawaii Volcanoes National Park

PO Box 52
Hawaii National Park, HI 96718
Phone: 808-985-6000

Hawaii Volcanoes National Park is on the island of Hawaii about 28 miles southwest of Hilo. It was established in 1916 and encompasses over 300,000 acres. Landscape features vary from sea level to the summit of the massive volcano, Mauna Loa at 13,677 feet. Over half of the park is designated wilderness and provides unusual hiking and camping opportunities. The park is open year-round. An entrance fee of $10 per vehicle is charged.

Park Activities

- ✓ Auto Touring
- Biking
- Boating
- ✓ Camping
- Climbing
- Fishing
- ✓ Hiking
- Horseback Riding
- Hunting
- Snow Skiing
- Swimming
- ✓ Wildlife Viewing

Information is available from the Kilauea Visitor Center, located just inside the park entrance. Videos highlighting the park's special features are shown in the auditorium. The visitor center is open daily from 7:45am to 5pm.

There are two drive-in campgrounds within the park. Campsites in both are available on a first-come, first-served basis. No camping fees are charged. Backcountry camping is by permit only.

Namakanipaio: located along HI 11 about 31 miles south of Hilo, open all year, restrooms, water, picnic tables, barbecue pits, seven day stay limit.

Kulanaokuaiki: located about five miles down Hilina Pali Road, open all year, eight sites, two are wheelchair accessible, vault toilets, picnic tables, seven day maximum stay. No water. Pets are not allowed.

Idaho

1 City of Rocks National Reserve
2 Craters of the Moon National Monument
3 Yellowstone National Park, see Wyoming

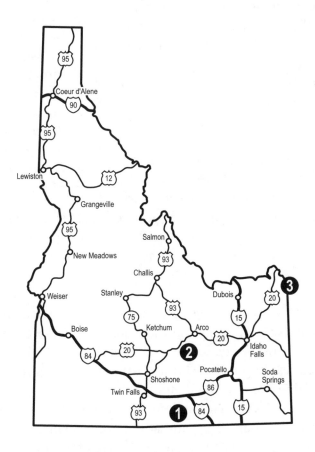

City of Rocks National Reserve

PO Box 169
Almo, ID 83312
Phone: 208-824-5910

City of Rocks National Reserve is in southern Idaho about 70 miles southeast of Twin Falls. The 14,407-acre park was established in 1988. Features include scenic granite spires and sculptured rock formations. Remnants of the California Trail are still visible in the area. There is no entrance fee.

Information is available from the visitor center in Almo. Brochures, climbing guides, historic trail information, camping information, books, and gifts are available. The center is open all year Monday through Friday from 8am to 4:30pm. It closes on winter holidays. The center remains open on weekends from mid-April to mid-October.

Park Activities
✓ Auto Touring
✓ Biking
Boating
✓ Camping
✓ Climbing
Fishing
✓ Hiking
✓ Horseback Riding
✓ Hunting
Snow Skiing
Swimming
✓ Wildlife Viewing

There are no developed campgrounds in City of Rocks National Reserve. About 64 designated campsites are scattered throughout the park; most are accessible from the road. Campsites are equipped with picnic tables and fire rings. Vault toilets are located throughout the Preserve. Potable water is available from the hand pump well located along Emery Canyon Road about one mile north of Bath Rock. Water is also available from the hand pump well at Bath Rock and at the visitor center. All other water should be treated before using. The camping fee for one vehicle and one site is $12.72 per night. An additional $8.48 is charged for an extra vehicle. A maximum of two vehicles, eight people, and two tents are allowed at a single site. Reservations are not required but are recommended from May through September; call 888-922-6743.

Craters of the Moon National Monument

PO Box 29
Arco, ID 83213
Phone: 208-527-1335

Craters of the Moon National Monument and Preserve is in central Idaho about 90 miles northeast of Twin Falls. It was established in 1924 and preserves more than 750,000 acres. The park contains more than 25 volcanic cones and 60 different lava flows. The monument is open year-round but winter snows limit automobile access around the Loop Drive and on roads within the park. An entrance fee of $8 per vehicle is charged.

Park Activities

✓ Auto Touring
✓ Biking
  Boating
✓ Camping
  Climbing
  Fishing
✓ Hiking
  Horseback Riding
✓ Hunting
  Snow Skiing
  Swimming
✓ Wildlife Viewing

Information is available from the Robert Limbert Visitor Center located just off US 20 about 25 miles northeast of Carey. It remains open all year except for winter holidays. A museum located inside the visitor center features exhibits that describe the natural and cultural history of the area.

There is one campground in the monument. All campsites are available on a first-come, first-served basis; no reservations are accepted. Wood fires are not permitted.

Lava Flow: located near the visitor center, open May through October, 51 sites, $10 per night in summer ($6 during off-season), picnic tables, grills, water, restrooms, 14 day maximum stay. Large RVs and trailers can be accommodated in a limited number of sites.

Indiana

1   Indiana Dunes National Lakeshore

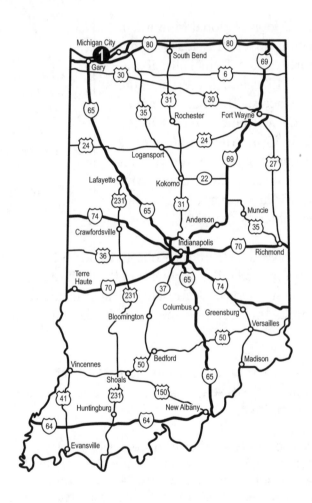

Indiana Dunes National Lakeshore

1100 N Mineral Springs Rd
Porter, IN 46304
Phone: 219-926-7561 ext 3

Indiana Dunes National Lakeshore is in northwest Indiana, just east of Gary. It encompasses nearly 25 miles of Lake Michigan shoreline between Gary and Michigan City. The national lakeshore was established in 1966 and contains over 15,000 acres. Features include miles of beaches, sand dunes, woodland forests, an 1830's French Canadian homestead, and a working 1900-era farm combine. There is no entrance fee.

Park Activities

✓ Auto Touring
✓ Biking
  Boating
✓ Camping
  Climbing
✓ Fishing
✓ Hiking
✓ Horseback Riding
  Hunting
✓ Snow Skiing
✓ Swimming
✓ Wildlife Viewing

Information is available from the visitor center in Porter on IN 49 about one mile north of I-94 Exit 26B. The visitor center is open daily except winter holidays. Features include a short orientation video, bookstore, and brochures describing the area's attractions.

There is one campground within the park. Campsites are available on a first-come, first-served basis; no reservations are accepted. Camping is also available in nearby Indiana Dunes State Park.

Dunewood: located off US 12 about five miles east of IN 49, open April through October, 53 drive-in sites, 25 walk-in sites, $15 per night, restrooms, hot showers, picnic tables, fire grates, no electric hookups, 14 day maximum stay.

Kentucky

1   Big South Fork National River & Recreation Area, see Tennessee
2   Cumberland Gap National Historical Park
3   Mammoth Cave National Park

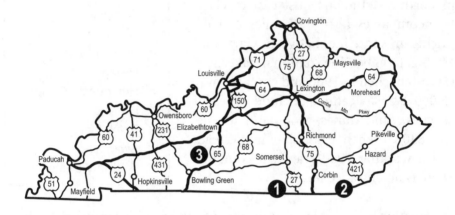

Cumberland Gap National Historical Park

91 Bartlett Park Rd
Middlesboro, KY 40965
Phone: 606-248-2817

Cumberland Gap National Historical Park is in southeast Kentucky, southwest Virginia, and northeastern Tennessee. The 20,454-acre park was established in 1940. This mountain pass developed into a main artery for settlers and was an important military objective in the Civil War. There is no entrance fee.

The park's visitor center is on US 25E just south of Middlesboro, Kentucky. The visitor center is open year-round (except Christmas Day) and features exhibits, artifacts, and two films depicting the history of the Gap.

Park Activities

- ✓ Auto Touring
- ✓ Biking
- Boating
- ✓ Camping
- Climbing
- Fishing
- ✓ Hiking
- ✓ Horseback Riding
- Hunting
- Snow Skiing
- Swimming
- ✓ Wildlife Viewing

One developed campground is available to visitors. Campsites are available on a first-come, first-served basis; reservations are not accepted. Backcountry camping is allowed in designated sites with a permit. Permits are free of charge and must be obtained at the visitor center.

Wilderness Road: located in Virginia along US 58 two miles east of US 25E, open all year, 160 sites, $12 per night, 41 sites have 30 and 50 amp electric hookups ($17 per night), hot showers, flush toilets, dump station, drinking water, picnic tables, fire grates, amphitheater, 14 day maximum stay.

Mammoth Cave National Park

PO Box 7
Mammoth Cave, KY 42259
Phone: 270-758-2180

Mammoth Cave National Park is in central Kentucky about 30 miles northeast of Bowling Green. The park was established in 1941 to preserve the longest recorded cave system in the world. It also preserves the scenic river valleys of the Green and Nolin Rivers. The park encompasses nearly 53,000 acres. There is no entrance fee. Cave tour fees range from $5 to $48.

Park Activities

✓ Auto Touring
✓ Biking
✓ Boating
✓ Camping
   Climbing
✓ Fishing
✓ Hiking
✓ Horseback Riding
   Hunting
   Snow Skiing
   Swimming
✓ Wildlife Viewing

Information is available from the visitor center located along Mammoth Cave Parkway, north of Park City. The center is open all year but hours vary by season. Features include exhibits of cave exploration, films, and a bookstore.

There are two developed campgrounds within the park. Reservations are recommended for sites in the Mammoth Cave Campground during peak season. Backcountry camping is allowed; a permit is required. Over a dozen backcountry sites are scattered along hiking trails. An equestrian campground is also available.

Mammoth Cave: located near the park's visitor center, open year-round, 105 sites (no hookups), $17 per night, dump station, picnic tables, fire grills, camp store, coin-operated showers, flush toilets, laundry facilities, drinking water, 14 day maximum stay. Reservations accepted (877-444-6777).

Houchin Ferry: primitive campground on the banks of Green River, located north of Brownsville along Houchins Ferry Road, 12 tent sites, $12 per night, picnic tables, fire grills, potable water, chemical toilets, 14 day maximum stay.

Maine

1   Acadia National Park

Acadia National Park

PO Box 177
Bar Harbor, ME 04609
Phone: 207-288-3338

Acadia National Park is in northern coastal Maine about 20 miles south of Ellsworth. It is the first national park east of the Mississippi. It contains 47,633 acres of granite-domed mountains, woodlands, lakes and ponds, and ocean shoreline. The park is open all year but some roads and attractions close in winter. An entrance fee of $20 is charged from late June to early October. May to late June and in October, the entrance fee is reduced to $10 per vehicle.

Park Activities

- ✓ Auto Touring
- ✓ Biking
- ✓ Boating
- ✓ Camping
- ✓ Climbing
- ✓ Fishing
- ✓ Hiking
- ✓ Horseback Riding
-    Hunting
- ✓ Snow Skiing
- ✓ Swimming
- ✓ Wildlife Viewing

Information is available from the Hulls Cove Visitor Center, which is open April to October. Information is available year-round from the park headquarters located along ME 233 near Eagle Lake. Thompson Island Information Center, located on the causeway at the head of Mount Desert Island, is open mid-May to mid-October; hours vary.

There are three campgrounds within the park. Duck Harbor Campground is remote and inaccessible to automobiles. The majority of sites in Blackwoods and Seawall Campgrounds are for tents but some sites can accommodate pop-ups, vehicle campers, and RVs up to 35 feet.

Blackwoods: located on ME 3 five miles south of Bar Harbor, open all year, 306 sites, $20 per night ($10 in April and November, free December through March), reservations suggested May through October (877-444-6777), restrooms, water, dump station, picnic tables, fire rings, 14 day maximum stay, 35-foot RV length limit. Showers and supply stores nearby. Limited facilities in winter.

Seawall: located on ME 102A four miles south of Southwest Harbor, open late May through September, 214 sites, $14 per night for walk-in sites, $20 per night for drive-in sites, restrooms, water, dump station, picnic tables, fire rings, 14 day maximum stay, 35-foot RV length limit. Showers and supply stores nearby. Reservations are accepted for approximately half of the campsites. Call 877-444-677 for reservation information. All other sites are available on a first-come, first-served basis.

Duck Harbor: located on Isle au Haut, inaccessible to automobiles, open mid-May to mid-October, five lean-to shelters, reservations required, $25 special use permit fee, picnic tables, fire rings, pit toilets, hand pump water. There is a three night stay limit from mid-June to mid-September; five day limit all other times.

Maryland

1 Assateague Island National Seashore
2 Catoctin Mountain Park
3 Chesapeake & Ohio Canal National Historical Park
4 Greenbelt Park

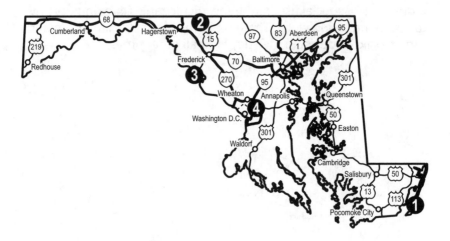

Assateague Island National Seashore

7206 National Seashore Ln
Berlin, MD 21811
Phone: 410-641-1441

Assateague Island National Seashore is in southeast Maryland, eight miles south of Ocean City. A portion also extends into Virginia but is managed by the Fish and Wildlife Service as Chincoteague National Wildlife Refuge. The national seashore was established in 1965 and encompasses 39,723 acres of land and water. An entrance fee of $15 per vehicle is charged.

Park Activities

Auto Touring
✓ Biking
✓ Boating
✓ Camping
Climbing
✓ Fishing
✓ Hiking
✓ Horseback Riding
✓ Hunting
Snow Skiing
✓ Swimming
✓ Wildlife Viewing

Information is available from the Assateague Island Visitor Center located along MD 611, before the Verrazzano Bridge entrance into the park. Features include beachcombing exhibits, educational brochures, nature films, and a marine aquarium. A visitor center is also in Chincoteague National Wildlife Refuge at Toms Cove.

There are both developed and primitive camping areas within the park. Camping is not available in the wildlife refuge. The State of Maryland manages nearby Assateague State Park, which has 350 campsites.

Developed: one oceanside and one bayside campground located eight miles south of Ocean City via MD 611, open all year, 90 RV/tent sites, 63 tent sites, cold showers, chemical toilets, drinking water, picnic tables, fire rings, dump station, 14 day maximum stay, 40-foot RV length limit. Campsites are available first-come, first-served from mid-October to mid-April and cost $20 per night. Reservations are recommended from mid-April to mid-October, call 877-444-6777. The camping fee during this time is $25 per night.

Primitive: open all year, chemical toilets, picnic tables, fire rings. A backcountry permit is required; the cost is $6. These sites are accessed by hiking or canoeing a distance of 2.5 to 13 miles from the ranger station.

Catoctin Mountain Park

6602 Foxville Rd
Thurmont, MD 21788
Phone: 301-663-9388

Park Activities
Auto Touring
Biking
Boating
✓ Camping
✓ Climbing
✓ Fishing
✓ Hiking
✓ Horseback Riding
Hunting
Snow Skiing
Swimming
✓ Wildlife Viewing

Catoctin Mountain Park is in northern Maryland about 20 miles east of Hagerstown. Originally established in 1936 as the Catoctin Recreational Demonstration Area, the 5,810-acre park was intended to provide recreational camps for employee groups. One of the camps eventually became the home of Presidential retreat, Camp David. Although Camp David is not open or accessible to the public, the eastern hardwood forest of Catoctin Mountain Park has many other attractions for visitors. No entrance fee is charged.

Information is available from the visitor center located on Park Central Road about four miles west of Thurmont. The center is open all year except holidays. A small exhibit area features native wildlife and cultural history.

There is one campground within the park. Rustic cabins are available for rent in Camp Misty Mount. A total of 28 cabins are available to individuals or groups. A grill, fire ring, and picnic table are located outside each cabin. Drinking water, hot showers, and flush toilets are centrally located.

Owens Creek: located two miles north of MD 77 via Foxville Deerfield Road, open May to November, 50 sites (3 pull-thru sites), $20 per night, picnic tables, grills, flush toilets, hot showers, 50-foot RV length limit (22 feet for travel trailers), seven day maximum stay. Campsites are available on a first-come, first-served basis; no reservations accepted. Pets allowed.

Chesapeake & Ohio Canal National Historical Park

1850 Dual Hwy, Ste 100
Hagerstown, MD 21740
Phone: 301-739-4200

Chesapeake and Ohio Canal National Historical Park runs through central Maryland. Portions also extend into the District of Columbia and West Virginia. The park follows the route of the Potomac River for 184.5 miles from Washington, D.C. to Cumberland, Maryland. Hundreds of original structures including locks, lockhouses, and aqueducts are among the park's features. An entrance fee of $5 per vehicle is charged at the Great Falls area. The entrance fee is valid for three days.

Park Activities

Auto Touring
✓ Biking
✓ Boating
✓ Camping
✓ Climbing
✓ Fishing
✓ Hiking
✓ Horseback Riding
Hunting
Snow Skiing
Swimming
✓ Wildlife Viewing

Six visitor centers are located throughout the park. All are open year-round but hours vary. The Brunswick Visitor Center is located at 40 West Potomac Street in Brunswick. Cumberland Visitor Center is in Cumberland at 13 Canal Street. Georgetown Visitor Center is in Washington, D.C. at 1057 Thomas Jefferson Street NW. The Great Falls Tavern Visitor Center is at 11710 MacArthur Boulevard in Potomac, Maryland. Hancock Visitor Center is in Hancock, Maryland, at 326 East Main Street. Williamsport Visitor Center is located at 205 West Potomac Street in Williamsport, Maryland. All have some type of exhibit on the canal's history as well as brochures.

There are three RV-accessible campgrounds, two walk-in, and 30 hiker/biker campgrounds. Hiker/biker campgrounds permit tent camping only and have pump well water and pit toilets. Length of stay is limited to one night in these campgrounds.

Antietam Creek: walk-in sites with parking adjacent to campground, located about 3 miles south of Sharpsburg via Harpers Ferry Rd, open all year, $10 per night, water, chemical toilets, 14 day maximum stay in summer, 30 day maximum stay rest of year. Campsites are available on a first-come, first-served basis only.

Fifteen Mile Creek: in Little Orleans east of Cumberland and south of I-68 via Orleans Road, open all year, ten RV/tent sites, $10 per night, primitive facilities, 14 day maximum stay in summer, 30 day maximum stay rest of year, 20-foot RV length limit. Campsites are available on a first-come, first-served basis only.

McCoys Ferry: located 15 miles west of Hagerstown and south of I-70 via MD 56 and McCoys Ferry Road, open all year, 14 RV/tent sites, $10 per night, primitive facilities, no drinking water, 14 day maximum stay in summer, 30 day maximum stay rest of year, 20-foot RV length limit. Campsites are available on a first-come, first-served basis.

Paw Paw: walk-in sites with parking adjacent to campground, located about 25 miles southeast of Cumberland via MD 51, open all year, $10 per night, water, chemical toilets, 14 day maximum stay in summer, 30 day maximum stay rest of year. Campsites are available on a first-come, first-served basis only.

Spring Gap: located eight miles south of Cumberland via MD 51, open all year, 20 RV/tent sites, $10 per night, primitive facilities, no drinking water, 14 day maximum stay in summer, 30 days rest of year, 20-foot RV length limit. Campsites are available on a first-come, first-served basis.

Greenbelt Park

6565 Greenbelt Rd
Greenbelt, MD 20770
Phone: 301-344-3948 or 301-344-3944

Greenbelt Park is in central Maryland about 25 miles southwest of Baltimore and 12 miles from Washington, D.C. It was established in 1950 and encompasses 1,176 acres. No entrance fee is charged.

Information is available from the park headquarters in Greenbelt along Greenbelt Road (MD 193). The office is open Monday through Friday from 8am to 4pm. Information is also available from the ranger station located near the campground entrance.

Park Activities
Auto Touring
✓ Biking
Boating
✓ Camping
Climbing
Fishing
✓ Hiking
✓ Horseback Riding
Hunting
Snow Skiing
Swimming
✓ Wildlife Viewing

There is one campground within the park. Campsite reservations can be made for summer months by calling 877-444-6777.

Greenbelt Park: located off Park Central Road south of main entrance, open all year, 174 RV/tent sites, $16 per night, hot showers, restrooms, dump station, picnic tables, playground, public phones, hiking trails, equestrian and bike trails nearby, 14 day maximum stay. There are no RV hookups.

Massachusetts

1 Boston Harbor Islands National Recreation Area

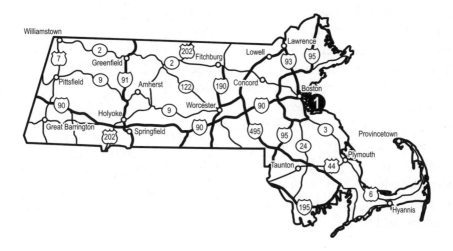

Boston Harbor Islands National Recreation Area

408 Atlantic Ave Ste 228
Boston, MA 02110
Phone: 617-223-8666

Boston Harbor Islands National Recreation Area is comprised of 34 islands situated within the Greater Boston shoreline. The islands are managed by a unique partnership of organizations, which includes the National Park Service and other public and private organizations. No entrance fee is charged. Passenger ferries connect to George's Island where water shuttles take visitors to other islands. The fare is $15 per person for adults, $11 for seniors, and $9 for children 3 to 11.

Park Activities
Auto Touring
Biking
✓ Boating
✓ Camping
Climbing
✓ Fishing
✓ Hiking
Horseback Riding
Hunting
Snow Skiing
✓ Swimming
✓ Wildlife Viewing

Information is available from the National Park Area Discovery Center located on Fan Pier at the United States Courthouse on South Boston's waterfront. Features include an interactive video, information desk, books and other island-related items for sale.

Primitive camping is available on four islands. Reservations and permits are required. There is a reservation fee charged in addtion to the camping fee. The Senior Pass and Access Pass is not accepted for discounts.

Bumpkin Island: located in Hingham Bay, open June to September, ten sites, no drinking water, pit toilets, 14 day maximum stay, reservations required (877-422-6762). Pets not allowed.

Grape Island: located in Hingham Bay, open June to September, ten sites, pit toilets, no drinking water, 14 day maximum stay, reservations required (877-422-6762). Pets not allowed.

Lovell's Island: located in Quincy Bay, open June to September, six sites, no drinking water, pit toilets, 14 day maximum stay, reservations required (877-422-6762). Pets not allowed.

Peddocks Island: Located in Hingham Bay, open June to September, six sites, no drinking water, pit toilets, 14 day maximum stay, reservations required (877-422-6762). Pets not allowed.

Michigan

1   Isle Royale National Park
2   Pictured Rocks National Lakeshore
3   Sleeping Bear Dunes National Lakeshore

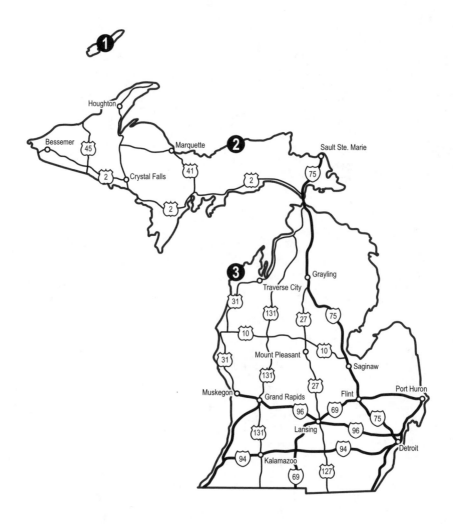

Isle Royale National Park

800 E Lakeshore Dr
Houghton, MI 49931
Phone: 906-482-0984

Isle Royale National Park is in extreme
northwest Michigan. This forested island
is the largest in Lake Superior. The park
was established in 1931 and encompasses
nearly 572,000 acres. No entrance fee is
charged but there is a user fee of $4 per
person, per day. Vehicles and wheeled
devices, except wheelchairs, are not
allowed on Isle Royale. The park is closed
November to mid-April.

Park Activities

Auto Touring
Biking
✓ Boating
✓ Camping
Climbing
✓ Fishing
✓ Hiking
Horseback Riding
Hunting
Snow Skiing
✓ Swimming
✓ Wildlife Viewing

Access to the island is by ferry. Visitors
can park their vehicles in Houghton or Copper Harbor, Michigan or in
Grand Portage, Minnesota. Visitors can also fly to the island via Royale
Air Service in Houghton, Michigan.

Three visitor centers provide information about the island and its
history. Houghton Visitor Center is located at 800 East Lakeshore Drive
in Houghton, Michigan. Rock Harbor Visitor Center is located in the
northeast section of the park in Rock Harbor. Windigo Visitor Center is
located in the southwest section of the park.

A total of 36 primitive campgrounds are available to visitors. Each may
contain individual tent sites, three-sided shelters, or group sites. A permit,
available free of charge, is required. Campgrounds are open mid-April
through October. No facilities are available at the campgrounds but hot
showers, groceries, and laundry facilities can be found in Rock Harbor
and Windigo. Campsites are available on a first-come, first-served basis
for parties of one to six; reservations are required for groups of seven to
ten people. No camping fee is charged. Rock Harbor Lodge offers motel-
style accommodations and self-contained cabins.

Beaver Island: three shelters, three night maximum stay, accessed by boat and canoe or kayak, campstoves only, no fires.

Belle Isle: one tent site, six shelters, five night maximum stay, fires permitted, boat and canoe or kayak access.

Birch Island: one tent site, one shelter, three night stay, boat and canoe or kayak access, campstoves only, no fires allowed.

Caribou Island: one tent site, two shelters, three night stay, boat and canoe or kayak access, fires permitted in community ring only.

Chickenbone East: three tent sites, one group site, two night stay limit, accessed by trail and canoe or kayak, campstoves only.

Chickenbone West: six tent sites, three group sites, two night stay limit, trail and canoe or kayak access, campstoves only.

Chippewa Harbor: two tent sites, four shelters, one group site, boat and canoe or kayak access, trail access, campfires permitted, three night stay limit.

Daisy Farm: six tent sites, 16 shelters, three group sites, three night stay limit, boat and canoe or kayak access, trail access, campstoves only.

Desor North: three tent sites, two night stay limit, campstoves only, trail access.

Desor South: seven tent sites, three group sites, two night stay limit, campstoves only, trail access.

Duncan Bay: one tent site, two shelters, three night maximum stay, boat and canoe or kayak access, campfires allowed.

Duncan Narrows: one tent site, two shelters, three night stay, boat and canoe or kayak access, campfires allowed.

Feldtmann Lake: five tent sites, two group sites, two night maximum stay, campstoves only, trail and canoe or kayak access.

Grace Island: two shelters, three night maximum stay, boat and canoe or kayak access, campstoves only.

Hatchet Lake: five tent sites, three group sites, two night stay limit, campstoves only, trail access.

Hay Bay: one tent site, three night stay limit, boat and canoe or kayak access, campstoves only.

Huginnin Cove: five tent sites, three night stay limit, canoe or kayak access, trail access, campstoves only.

Intermediate Lake: three tent sites, two night maximum stay, canoe or kayak access, campstoves only.

Island Mine: four tent sites, two group sites, three night stay, campfires allowed, trail access.

Lake Richie: four tent sites, two group sites, two night stay limit, canoe or kayak access, trail access, campstoves only.

Lake Richie Canoe: three tent sites, two night stay, canoe or kayak access, campstoves only.

Lake Whittlesey: three tent sites, two night stay limit, canoe or kayak access, campstoves only.

Lane Cove: five tent sites, three night maximum stay, canoe or kayak access, trail access, campstoves only.

Little Todd: four tent sites, two night stay limit, campfires allowed, trail and canoe or kayak access.

Malone Bay: five shelters, two group sites, three night maximum stay, boat and canoe or kayak access, trail access, campfires permitted.

McCargoe Cove: three tent sites, six shelters, three group sites, three night stay, boat and canoe or kayak access, trail access, campfires permitted in community ring only.

Merritt Lane: one tent site, one shelter, three night stay limit, boat and canoe or kayak access, campstoves only.

Moskey Basin: two tent sites, six shelters, two group sites, three night stay, boat and canoe or kayak access, trail access, campstoves only.

Pickerel Cove: one tent site, two night maximum stay, canoe or kayak access, campstoves only.

Rock Harbor: 11 tent sites, nine shelters, three group sites, one day stay limit, boat and canoe or kayak access, trail access, treated water supply, campstoves only.

Siskiwit Bay: four tent sites, two shelters, three group sites, three night stay, boat and canoe or kayak access, trail access, campfires allowed in community ring only.

Three Mile: four tent sites, eight shelters, three group sites, one night stay limit, boat and canoe or kayak access, trail access, campstoves only.

Todd Harbor: five tent sites, one shelter, three group sites, three night stay limit, boat and canoe or kayak access, trail access, campfires permitted in community ring only.

Tookers Island: two shelters, three night stay limit, access by boat and canoe or kayak, campstoves only.

Washington Creek: five tent sites, ten shelters, four group sites, three night stay, canoe or kayak access, trail access, treated water supply, campstoves only.

Wood Lake: three tent sites, two night maximum stay, campstoves only, canoe or kayak access.

Pictured Rocks National Lakeshore

PO Box 40
Munising, MI 49862
Phone: 906-387-3700

Pictured Rocks National Lakeshore is in northern Michigan between Munising and Grand Marais. The park was authorized in 1966 and encompasses 73,235 acres. Features include sandstone cliffs, long beach strands, sand dunes, waterfalls, inland lakes, wetlands, and hardwood forests. No entrance fee is charged.

Information is available year-round from the Pictured Rocks National Lakeshore/ Hiawatha National Forest Interagency Visitor Center in Munising at the junction of Michigan Highway M-28 and County Road H-58. In summer, information is available from the Grand Sable Visitor Center, Miners Castle Information Center, and Munising Falls Interpretive Center.

Park Activities
Auto Touring
Biking
✓ Boating
✓ Camping
Climbing
✓ Fishing
✓ Hiking
Horseback Riding
✓ Hunting
Snow Skiing
✓ Swimming
✓ Wildlife Viewing

There are three drive-in campgrounds within the park. All campsites are available on a first-come, first-served basis. Several primitive hike-in campgrounds are also available; a permit is required.

Hurricane River: located off Alger County Road H-58 12 miles west of Grand Marais, open mid-May through October, 21 sites, $14 per night, picnic tables, fire grills, water, vault toilets, 36-foot RV length limit (42 feet vehicle/trailer combination), 14 day maximum stay.

Little Beaver Lake: located 20 miles northeast of Munising off Alger County Road H-58, open mid-May through October, eight sites, $14 per night, nature trail, boat ramp, picnic tables, fire grills, water, vault toilets, 14 day maximum stay. Single unit vehicles in excess of 36 feet and vehicle/trailer combined units in excess of 42 feet are prohibited because of the small campsites and the narrow, twisting, hilly access road.

Twelvemile Beach: located 15 miles west of Grand Marais off County Road H-58, open mid-May through October, 36 sites, $14 per night (lakeside sites are $16 per night), picnic tables, fire grills, vault toilets, water, nature trail, 14 day stay limit. Because the turning radius and some parking site lengths are limited within the campground, single unit vehicles in excess of 36 feet and vehicle/trailer combined units in excess of 42 feet are not recommened in the campground.

Sleeping Bear Dunes National Lakeshore

9922 Front St
Empire, MI 49630
Phone: 231-326-5134

Sleeping Bear Dunes National Lakeshore is in central Michigan about 24 miles west of Traverse City. The park encompasses a 35-mile stretch of Lake Michigan's eastern coastline. Established in 1977, the park features hardwood forests, beaches, sand dunes, and steep bluffs. An entrance fee of $10 is charged.

Information is available from the Philip A. Hart Visitor Center located on highway M-72 in Empire. The center is open all year. Exhibits describe the history of the area. Information is also available from ranger stations in both campgrounds.

Park Activities

✓ Auto Touring
Biking
✓ Boating
✓ Camping
Climbing
✓ Fishing
✓ Hiking
Horseback Riding
✓ Hunting
Snow Skiing
✓ Swimming
✓ Wildlife Viewing

There are two developed campgrounds within the park. Backcountry camping is also available and requires the purchase of a permit ($5 per night).

D.H. Day: located two miles west of Glen Arbor off MI 109, open April through November, 88 sites, $12 per night, 14 day stay limit, dump station, vault toilets, water, public phone, amphitheater, handicap-accessible site. Campsites available first-come, first-served; reservations not accepted.

Platte River: located nine miles south of Empire via MI 22, open all year, 96 sites with 30-amp electric hookups ($21 per night), 53 sites without electricity ($16 per night), 25 walk-in sites ($12 per night), some pull-thrus, reservations accepted (877-444-6777), picnic tables, drinking water, hot showers, flush toilets, amphitheater, dump station, trails, public phones, 14 day maximum stay.

Minnesota

Grand Portage National Monument

PO Box 426
Grand Portage, MN 55605
Phone: 218-475-0123

Grand Portage National Monument is in northeast Minnesota about 35 miles northeast of Grand Marais. Established in 1951, the park preserves a vital headquarters of 18th, 19th, and 20th century fur trade activity and Ojibwe heritage. No entrance fee is charged.

Information is available at the Heritage Center located at 170 Mile Creek Road in Grand Portage. The center is open year-round and features exhibits about Ojibwe culture and the fur trade, a book store, and multi-media programs.

Park Activities
Auto Touring
Biking
Boating
✓ Camping
Climbing
✓ Fishing
✓ Hiking
Horseback Riding
Hunting
Snow Skiing
Swimming
✓ Wildlife Viewing

Camping is permitted in the monument at Fort Charlotte on the Pigeon River, which is reached by hiking the Grand Portage 8.5 miles from the historic stockade or four miles from the crossing at Old Highway 61.

> **Fort Charlotte**: two primitive sites that can accommodate up to ten people, picnic tables, fire pits, pit toilets, no charge for camping but a free backcountry permit is required. Water from the Pigeon River or Snow Creek is not potable; it should be treated before consuming.

Voyageurs National Park

360 Highway 11 East
International Falls, MN 56649
Phone: 218-286-5258 or 888-381-2873

Voyageurs National Park is located in northern Minnesota, 15 miles east of International Falls. Established in 1975, the 218,054-acre park was once the route of the French-Canadian voyageurs. The park remains open year-round. No entrance fee is charged.

Three visitor centers provide information about the park and its history. Ash River Visitor Center is about 40 miles southeast of International Falls via US 53 and CR 129. Kabetogama Lake Visitor Center is 24 miles southeast of International Falls via US 53 and CR 122. Rainy Lake Visitor Center is open year-round and is ten miles east of International Falls off MN 11.

There are more than 200 individual tent camping, houseboat, and day use sites throughout the park. Designated tent sites have a mooring aid, tent pad, fire ring, privy, picnic table, and bear-proof food storage locker. Houseboat sites include two mooring aids and a fire ring. There are no camping fees but a permit is required, which is available for free at the visitor centers. Campsites are available on a first-come, first-served basis.

Park Activities

Auto Touring
Biking
✓ Boating
✓ Camping
Climbing
✓ Fishing
✓ Hiking
Horseback Riding
Hunting
✓ Snow Skiing
✓ Swimming
✓ Wildlife Viewing

Mississippi

1   Gulf Islands National Seashore, see Florida
2   Natchez Trace Parkway

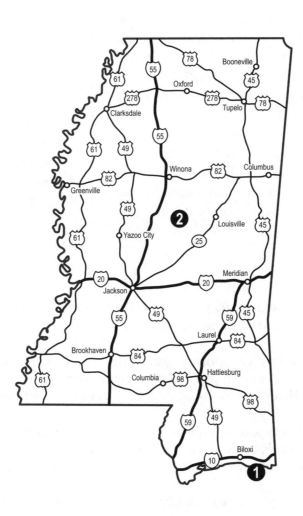

Natchez Trace Parkway

2680 Natchez Trace Parkway
Tupelo, MS 38804
Phone: 800-305-7417

Natchez Trace Parkway is a 444-mile route across Mississippi, Alabama, and Tennessee. It generally follows the trace, or trail, used by American Indians and early settlers. The parkway was established in 1938.

Information is available from the visitor center in Tupelo at Milepost 266. Several remote contact stations are located along the parkway. The visitor center is open daily between 8am and 5pm except Christmas Day.

Park Activities
✓ Auto Touring
✓ Biking
✓ Boating
✓ Camping
Climbing
✓ Fishing
✓ Hiking
✓ Horseback Riding
Hunting
Snow Skiing
✓ Swimming
✓ Wildlife Viewing

There are three National Park Service campgrounds along Natchez Trace Parkway. Camping is also available in numerous public and private campgrounds located along the parkway.

Jeff Busby: in Mississippi at milepost 193.1 about 12 miles south of Mathiston, open all year, 18 sites, no camping fee, picnic tables, nature trail, restrooms, public phone, 14 day maximum stay.

Meriwether Lewis: in Tennessee at milepost 385.9 about seven miles east of Hohenwald, open all year, 32 sites, no camping fee, picnic tables, restrooms, nature trails, 14 day maximum stay.

Rocky Springs: in Mississippi at milepost 54.8 about 15 miles northeast of Port Gibson, open all year, 22 sites, no camping fee, picnic tables, restrooms, nature trails, public phone, 14 day maximum stay.

Missouri

1   Ozark National Scenic Riverways

Ozark National Scenic Riverways

PO Box 490
Van Buren, MO 63965
Phone: 573-323-4236

Ozark National Scenic Riverways protects
134 miles of the Current and Jacks Fork
rivers in southeast Missouri. The park
was established in 1964 and encompasses
80,790 acres. No entrance fee is charged.

Information can be obtained from park
headquarters in Van Buren. The office is
located just east of town at 404 Watercress
Drive and is open all year, Monday through
Friday from 8am to 4:30pm (closed on
holidays). Features include exhibits on

Park Activities
✓ Auto Touring
✓ Biking
✓ Boating
✓ Camping
Climbing
✓ Fishing
✓ Hiking
✓ Horseback Riding
✓ Hunting
Snow Skiing
✓ Swimming
✓ Wildlife Viewing

the resources and history of the Ozarks, informational brochures, and
books.

There are six developed campgrounds available to visitors. Campsite
reservations can be made by calling 877-444-6777. There are several
primitive camping areas also within the park. These cost $5 per night
and can accommodate two tents and up to six people. Camping is also
available in Montauk State Park.

Alley Spring: located six miles west of Eminence off MO 106, open
all year, 162 sites (some with 50 amp electric hookups), $17 per
night for non-electric sites, $20 for sites with electric hookups, 14
day maximum stay, hot showers, flush toilets, dump station, river
access. Water is not available from November to mid-April. Pets
allowed.

Big Spring: located four miles south of Van Buren off MO 103,
open all year, 123 sites, $17 per night for non-electric sites, $20 for
sites with electric hookups, 14 day maximum stay, hot showers,
flush toilets, dump station, river access. Water is not available from
November to mid-April. Pets allowed.

Powder Mill: located 19 miles west of Ellington via MO 106, open all year, eight sites (no hookups), $17 per night, reservations not accepted.

Pulltite: 24 miles north of Eminence via State Highways 19 and EE, open all year, 55 campsites (no hookups), $17 per night, 14 day maximum stay, flush toilets, showers, river access. Water is not available from November to mid-April. Pets allowed.

Round Spring: located off MO 19 about 16 miles north of Eminence, open all year, 60 campsites (some with 50 amp electric hookups), $17 per night for non-electric sites, $20 for sites with electric hookups, 14 day maximum stay, hot showers, dump station, flush toilets, river access, cave tours (fee charged). Water is not available from November to mid-April. Pets allowed.

Two Rivers: located seven miles east of Eminence via State Highways 106 and V, open all year, 19 sites, $17 per night (mid-April to mid-October), flush toilets, showers, 14 day maximum stay, river access. Water is not available from November to mid-April. Pets allowed. Reservations accepted only for group sites.

Montana

1   Bighorn Canyon National Recreation Area
2   Glacier National Park
3   Yellowstone National Park, see Wyoming

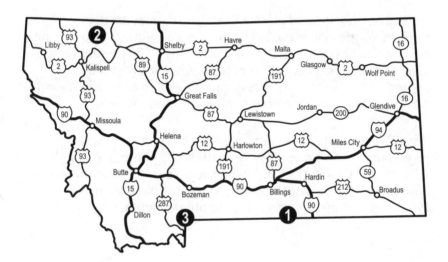

Bighorn Canyon National Recreation Area

PO Box 7458
Fort Smith, MT 59035
Phone: 307-548-5406

Bighorn Canyon National Recreation Area is in south-central Montana and northern Wyoming. The park was established in 1966 and contains over 120,000 acres. The north and south ends are not connected by a direct road. Access to the north end is via MT 313 south of Hardin. The south end is accessed from US 14A near Lovell, Wyoming. An entrance fee of $5 is charged.

Park Activities
✓ Auto Touring
✓ Biking
✓ Boating
✓ Camping
Climbing
✓ Fishing
✓ Hiking
Horseback Riding
✓ Hunting
Snow Skiing
✓ Swimming
✓ Wildlife Viewing

Information is available from two visitor centers. Bighorn Canyon Visitor Center in Lovell, Wyoming, is open year-round. Among the exhibits is a relief map of Bighorn Canyon and the surrounding area. Yellowtail Dam Visitor Center is in the northern part of the park near Fort Smith, Montana, and is open May through September.

There are five campgrounds in Bighorn Canyon National Recreation Area. Campsites are available on a first-come, first-served basis; reservations are not accepted. Black Canyon and Medicine Creek are boat-in campgrounds.

Afterbay: in Montana about 42 miles south of Hardin off MT 313, open all year, 28 RV/tent sites, no camping fee, picnic tables, grills, bear-proof food containers, vault toilets, boat ramp, drinking water, dump station, 14 day maximum stay. An additional 12 sites without water are available on the north shore of the Afterbay.

Black Canyon: boat-in campground located five miles south of Ok-A-Beh Marina at dayboard 5, 17 tent sites, no camping fee, picnic tables, grills, bear-proof food storage, floating vault toilets, no drinking water. Lake level affects the proximity of boat moorings to campsites.

Horseshoe Bend: in Wyoming about 14 miles north of Lovell off WY 37, open all year, 29 sites without hookups (no camping fee), 19 sites (3 pull-thru) with water and electric hookups ($15 per night), picnic tables, grills, flush toilets, boat ramp, drinking water, dump station, 14 day maximum stay. The Senior Pass and Access Pass provide free entrance into the NRA but are not accepted to discount the utility fee.

Medicine Creek: boat-in or hike-in campground north of Barry's Landing at dayboard 32, open year-round, six tent sites, no camping fee, picnic tables, grills, floating vault toilet, boat docks, no drinking water. Lake level affects the proximity of boat moorings to campsites.

Trail Creek: located along Barry's Landing Road off WY 37, open all year, 15 sites (5 tent only sites), no camping fee, 16-foot RV length limit, 14 day maximum stay, picnic tables, grills, bear-proof food storage, vault toilets, boat ramp nearby, no drinking water.

Glacier National Park

PO Box 128
West Glacier, MT 59936
Phone: 406-888-7800

Glacier National Park is in northwest
Montana about 140 miles north of
Missoula. The park was established in
1910 and preserves over one million acres
of mountains and glaciers. An entrance fee
of $25 is charged May through October;
$15 the rest of the year.

Visitor centers are located in Apgar,
Logan Pass, and Saint Mary. Park rangers
on duty throughout summer months. In
winter, Apgar Visitor Center is open on
weekends. It is located two miles north of West Glacier, the western
entrance to the park. Logan Pass Visitor Center is along the Going-to-
the-Sun Road and the Saint Mary Visitor Center is located just west of
Saint Mary off US 89.

Park Activities
✓ Auto Touring
✓ Biking
✓ Boating
✓ Camping
Climbing
✓ Fishing
✓ Hiking
✓ Horseback Riding
Hunting
Snow Skiing
Swimming
✓ Wildlife Viewing

Glacier National Park has 13 campgrounds. Most campsites are
available on a first-come, first-served basis. Fish Creek and Saint Mary
Campgrounds have sites that may be reserved by calling 877-444-6777.
Utility hookups are not available in any campground. Backcountry
camping is allowed; a permit, available for free, is required.

Apgar: two miles north of West Glacier off Going-to-the-Sun Road,
open May to October, 194 sites, $20 per night, 40-foot RV length
limit, flush toilets, dump station, hiker/biker sites available, seven
day maximum stay. Primitive camping allowed during the off-
season.

Avalanche: on Going-to-the-Sun Road about 15 miles northeast of
West Glacier, open June to September, 87 sites, $20 per night, 26-
foot RV length limit, flush toilets, hiker/biker sites available, seven
day maximum stay.

Bowman Lake: 30 miles northwest of West Glacier and six miles east of Polebridge via North Fork Road, open May to September, 48 sites, $15 per night, pit toilets nearby, potable water, seven day maximum stay. Campground access road is a narrow and windy dirt road; RVs are not recommended. Primitive camping allowed during the off-season.

Cut Bank: located ten miles northwest of Kiowa via US 89 and dirt road, open June to September, 14 sites, $10 per night, pit toilets, no water, seven day maximum stay. Campground access road is dirt; RVs not recommended.

Fish Creek: off Camas Creek Road four miles north of West Glacier, open June to September, 178 sites, $23 per night, 35-foot RV length limit, flush toilets, coin-operated showers, dump station, reservations accepted (877-444-6777), seven day maximum stay.

Kintla Lake: located about 43 miles north of West Glacier via North Fork Road, open May to September, 13 sites, $15 per night, potable water, pit toilets, seven day stay limit. Campground access road is a narrow and windy dirt road; RVs not recommended. Primitive camping allowed during the off-season.

Logging Creek: north of West Glacier along North Fork Road, open July to September, seven sites, $10 per night, pit toilets, no water, seven day stay limit. Campground access road is a narrow and windy dirt road; RVs not recommended.

Many Glacier: located 12 miles west of Babb on Many Glacier Road, open May to September, 110 sites, $20 per night, 35-foot RV length limit, potable water, flush toilets, dump station, hiker/biker sites available, seven day stay limit. Primitive camping allowed during the off-season.

Quartz Creek: north of West Glacier along North Fork Road, open July to October, seven sites, $10 per night, pit toilets, no water, seven day maximum stay. Road to campground is a narrow and windy dirt road; RVs not recommended.

Rising Sun: six miles west of Saint Mary on Going-to-the-Sun Road, open May to September, 83 sites, $20 per night, 25-foot RV length limit, potable water, flush toilets, coin-operated showers, dump station, hiker/biker sites available, camp store and restaurant nearby, seven day maximum stay.

Sprague Creek: on Going-to-the-Sun Road ten miles north of West Glacier, open May to September, 25 sites, $20 per night, no towed units permitted, potable water, flush toilets, seven day maximum stay. Camp store, restaurant, gift shop, tour buses, boat rides, and horse rides available at nearby McDonald Lodge.

Saint Mary: just west of Saint Mary along Going-to-the-Sun Road, open May to September, 148 sites, $23 per night, 35-foot RV length limit, potable water, flush toilets, coin-operated showers, dump station, reservations accepted (877-444-6777), hiker/biker sites available, seven day maximum stay. Primitive camping allowed during the off-season.

Two Medicine: 13 miles northwest of East Glacier Park via MT 49 and Two Medicine Road, open May to September, 99 sites, $20 per night, 32-foot RV length limit, potable water, flush toilets, dump station, hiker/biker sites available, seven day maximum stay. Camp store and gift shop nearby. Primitive camping allowed during the off-season.

Nevada

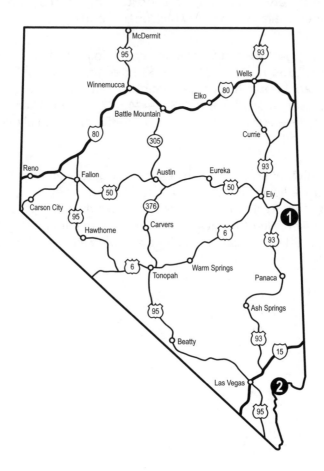

Great Basin National Park

100 Great Basin National Park
Baker, NV 89311
Phone: 775-234-7331

Great Basin National Park is in east-central Nevada about 60 miles east of Ely. The park was established in 1986 and encompasses 77,180 acres. Features include streams, lakes, alpine plants, ancient bristlecone pines, and numerous limestone caverns, including Lehman Caves. No entrance fee is charged. Cave tour fees vary from $8 to $10 for adults.

Park Activities
✓ Auto Touring
✓ Biking
Boating
✓ Camping
Climbing
✓ Fishing
✓ Hiking
✓ Horseback Riding
Hunting
Snow Skiing
Swimming
✓ Wildlife Viewing

Information is available from the Great Basin Visitor Center, located just north of the town of Baker on the west side of NV 487. The visitor center is open daily in summer. Information is also available at the Lehman Caves Visitor Center year-round, which is in the park about five miles west of Baker on NV 488.

There are five devloped campgrounds within the park. All campsites are available on a first-come, first-served basis. A dump station ($5 fee) is located near the Lehman Caves Visitor Center. Primitive camping areas are located along Snake Creek and Strawberry Creek Roads; sites have picnic tables and fire rings.

Baker Creek: three miles south of Lehman Caves Visitor Center on Baker Creek Road, open May to October, 34 campsites, some pull-thru sites, $12 per night, pit toilets, water available in summer only, 30-foot RV length limit, 14 day maximum stay.

Lower Lehman Creek: two miles from Lehman Caves Visitor Center on Wheeler Peak Scenic Drive, open all year, 11 sites, some pull-thru sites, $12 per night, pit toilets, water available in summer only, 42-foot RV length limit, 14 day maximum stay.

Upper Lehman Creek: three miles from Lehman Caves Visitor Center along Wheeler Peak Scenic Drive, open April to October, 22 campsites, $12 per night, pit toilets, water available in summer only, 36-foot RV length limit, 14 day maximum stay.

Strawberry Creek: located on Strawberry Creek Rd about three miles south of US 50, open all year, eight sites (two walk-in), no camping fee, pit toilets, no drinking water is available, 14 day stay limit. Campground access road is a primitive dirt road.

Wheeler Peak: located 12 miles from Lehman Caves Visitor Center at the end of Wheeler Peak Scenic Drive, open June to October, 37 campsites, $12 per night, 24-foot RV length limit, pit toilets, water available only in summer, 14 day maximum stay. The road to this campground is narrow, curvy, and climbs an eight percent grade in 12 miles. RVs and vehicles pulling trailers are not recommended.

Lake Mead National Recreation Area

601 Nevada Way
Boulder City, NV 89005
Phone: 702-293-8990

Lake Mead National Recreation Area is in southeast Nevada and northwest Arizona. It was established in 1964 and encompasses nearly 1.5 million acres. Features include Lake Mead (formed by Hoover Dam), Lake Mohave (formed by Davis Dam on the Colorado River), and over one million acres of surrounding desert and mountains. An entrance fee of $5 is charged.

Park Activities

✓ Auto Touring
✓ Biking
✓ Boating
✓ Camping
  Climbing
✓ Fishing
✓ Hiking
✓ Horseback Riding
✓ Hunting
  Snow Skiing
✓ Swimming
✓ Wildlife Viewing

Information is available from the Lake Mead Visitor Center located east of Boulder City off US 93. The visitor center features a relief map of the park and a geology exhibit. Information is also available from various information stations and contact stations.

There are seven National Park Service campgrounds throughout the recreation area. All campsites are available on a first-come, first-served basis; reservations are not accepted. Concession-operated campgrounds that have campsites with hookups are also available. Backcountry camping is permitted.

Boulder Beach: six miles north of Boulder City off NV 166, open all year, 154 RV/tent sites, $10 per night, 30 day stay limit, restrooms, water, dump station, grills, picnic tables.

Callville Bay: 22 miles northeast of Henderson via NV 147 and NV 167, open all year, 80 sites, $10 per night, 30 day maximum stay, restrooms, water, dump station, grills, picnic tables.

Cottonwood Cove: on Lake Mohave 14 miles east of Searchlight on NV 164, open all year, 145 RV/tent sites in two campgrounds,

$10 per night, restrooms, water, dump station, grills, picnic tables, 30 day stay limit in upper campground, 15 day limit in lower campground.

Echo Bay: 30 miles south of Overton via NV 169 and NV 167, open all year, 166 RV/tent sites, $10 per night, 30 day maximum stay, restrooms, water, dump station, grills, picnic tables.

Katherine Landing: in Arizona five miles north of Bullhead City off AZ 68, open all year, 173 RV/tent sites, $10 per night, 30 day maximum stay, restrooms, water, dump station, grills, picnic tables.

Las Vegas Bay: eight miles northeast of Henderson off NV 147, open all year, 89 sites, $10 per night, 30 day maximum stay, restrooms, water, dump station, grills, picnic tables.

Temple Bar: in Arizona 80 miles north of Kingman via US 93, open all year, 153 RV/tent sites, $10 per night, 30 day maximum stay, restrooms, water, dump station, grills, picnic tables.

New Mexico

1   Bandelier National Monument
2   Carlsbad Caverns National Park
3   Chaco Culture National Historical Park
4   El Malpais National Monument
5   El Morro National Monument

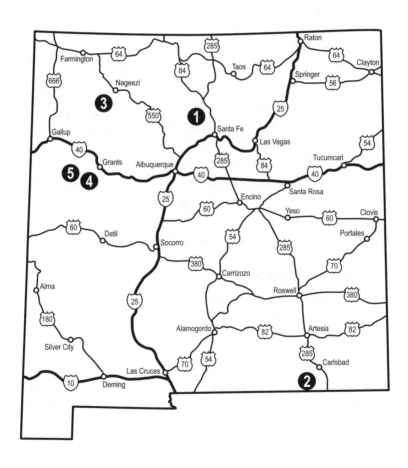

Bandelier National Monument

15 Entrance Rd
Los Alamos, NM 87544
Phone: 505-672-3861 ext. 517

Bandelier National Monument is in north-central New Mexico about 40 miles west of Santa Fe. The national monument protects Pueblo Indian cliff houses and villages on mesa tops and canyon walls. The 33,676-acre park was established in 1916. An entrance fee of $12 is charged.

Information is available from the visitor center located off NM 4 in Frijoles Canyon, about three miles from the park entrance. The visitor center is open all year except on December 25 and January 1. Features include exhibits on the Pueblo Indian culture. Because of severe space limitations, trailers may not be brought into the parking areas in Frijoles Canyon (drop them off at Juniper Campground, near the park entrance).

There is one campground in the monument. Sites are available on a first-come, first-served basis; reservations are not accepted (the campground seldom fills). Backcountry camping requires a permit, available for free at the visitor center. Pets are not permitted on trails.

> **Juniper**: located on the mesa top near the park entrance, open year-round depending on weather, 94 RV/tent sites, $12 per night, picnic tables, fire grills, water, flush toilets, dump station, 14 day maximum stay, 41-foot RV length limit.

Park Activities

Auto Touring
Biking
Boating
✓ Camping
Climbing
Fishing
✓ Hiking
Horseback Riding
Hunting
Snow Skiing
Swimming
✓ Wildlife Viewing

Carlsbad Caverns National Park

3225 National Parks Highway
Carlsbad, NM 88220
Phone: 575-785-2232

Carlsbad Caverns National Park is in southeast New Mexico about 20 miles south of Carlsbad. It was established in 1923 and encompasses 46,766 acres. It preserves Carlsbad Cavern and numerous other caves. The park contains more than 100 known caves. An entrance fee of $6 per person is charged. Fees for cave tours vary from $7 to $20.

Park Activities

Auto Touring
Biking
Boating
✓ Camping
Climbing
Fishing
✓ Hiking
Horseback Riding
Hunting
Snow Skiing
Swimming
✓ Wildlife Viewing

Information is available from the Carlsbad Caverns Visitor Center, located seven miles from the park entrance near White's City on US 62/180. It remains open year-round. The visitor center features exhibits on bats, geology, cave restoration, and park history.

There are no developed campgrounds within the park. Backcountry camping requires a permit that is available for free at the visitor center. Camping is allowed in designated wilderness areas only. Campsites must be at least one-half mile away from roads, 300 feet from any natural water source or cave entrance, and 100 feet off established trails. Campfires are not permitted within the park; use only campstoves. Entering backcountry caves without written permission of the superintendent is prohibited.

Chaco Culture National Historical Park

PO Box 220
Nageezi, NM 87037
Phone: 505-786-7014 ext 221

Chaco Culture National Historical Park is in northwest New Mexico about 70 miles southeast of Farmington. The park encompasses nearly 34,000 acres and was originally established in 1907 as the Chaco Canyon National Monument. The park contains 13 major prehistoric sites and hundreds of smaller ones built by the Ancestral Puebloan People. The entrance fee is $8 per vehicle.

Park Activities

Auto Touring
✓ Biking
Boating
✓ Camping
Climbing
Fishing
✓ Hiking
Horseback Riding
Hunting
Snow Skiing
Swimming
✓ Wildlife Viewing

Information is available from the visitor center located 24 miles south of Nageezi. Getting to the park and visitor center can be a little difficult. The recommended route from Nageezi is to follow US 550 south three miles to CR 7900 and then CR 7950. You'll encounter eight miles of paved road (CR 7900) and thirteen miles of dirt road. The visitor center is a few miles from the park entrance. The center is open all year (except Thanksgiving, Christmas Day, and New Year's Day) and has exhibits on the cultural history of Chaco Canyon.

There is one campground in the park. Campsites are available on a first-come, first-served basis; reservations are not accepted. Gathering wood is prohibited and no firewood is available in the park; bring in what you may need.

Gallo: located one mile east of the visitor center, open year-round, 49 sites, $10 per night, picnic tables, fire grate, flush toilets, dump station, drinking water available at visitor center, 35-foot RV length limit, 7 day maximum stay. Pets are allowed.

El Malpais National Monument

123 E Roosevelt Ave
Grants, NM 87020
Phone: 505-783-4774

Park Activities

✓ Auto Touring
✓ Biking
  Boating
✓ Camping
✓ Climbing
  Fishing
✓ Hiking
✓ Horseback Riding
  Hunting
  Snow Skiing
  Swimming
✓ Wildlife Viewing

El Malpais National Monument is in west-central New Mexico about 75 miles west of Albuquerque. The park was established in 1987 and encompasses 114,277 acres. El Malpais is a spectacular volcanic area, featuring cinder cones, a 17-mile-long lava tube system, and ice caves. El Malpais is managed jointly by the National Park Service and Bureau of Land Management. No entrance fee is charged.

Information is available from El Malpais Information Center, which is located 23 miles south of Grants on NM 53. The center is open all year from 8:30am to 4:30pm except Thanksgiving Day, Christmas Day, and New Year's Day. Rangers conduct a variety of programs, hikes, and demonstrations during summer. Information can also be obtained at the Northwest New Mexico Visitor Center on I-40 at Exit 85.

There are no developed National Park Service campgrounds within the park. Backcountry camping is allowed in some areas; a free permit is required and may be obtained at the information center. The Bureau of Land Management manages the campground described below.

> **Joe Skeen**: located 11 miles south of I-40 Exit 89 along NM 117, open all year, 10 sites, some pull-thrus, no camping fee, picnic tables, fire rings, vault toilets, 50-foot RV limit, 14-day stay limit. Reservations are not accepted.

El Morro National Monument

HC 61 Box 43
Ramah, NM 87321
Phone: 505-783-4226

El Morro National Monument is in west-central New Mexico, 43 miles southwest of Grants along NM 53. Established in 1906, the 1,278-acre monument features "Inscription Rock," upon which are carved about two thousand inscriptions from early travelers. The monument also includes petroglyphs and Pueblo Indian ruins. An entrance fee of $3 per person (16 and over) is charged.

Park Activities

Auto Touring
Biking
Boating
✓ Camping
Climbing
Fishing
✓ Hiking
Horseback Riding
Hunting
Snow Skiing
Swimming
✓ Wildlife Viewing

Information is available from the visitor center located along the entrance road. The center is open year-round. Features include a brief video about the park and a museum.

There is one small campground in the monument. Campsites are available on a first-come, first-served basis. Facilities are limited in winter (water is shut off). There is no camping fee in winter.

El Morro: located along entrance road off NM 53, open all year, nine sites, $5 per night, picnic tables, drinking water, fire grills, pit toilets, 27-foot RV length limit, 14 day maximum stay, no hookups.

New York

1   Fire Island National Seashore

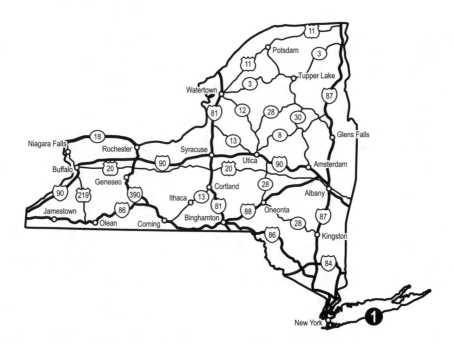

Fire Island National Seashore

120 Laurel St
Patchogue, NY 11772
Phone: 631-687-4750

Fire Island National Seashore is in southeast New York about 60 miles east of New York City. Established in 1964, the 19,578-acre park features beaches, dunes, Fire Island Lighthouse, and the nearby estate of William Floyd, a signer of the Declaration of Independence. No entrance fee is charged.

There are no public roads on the island itself; getting around requires walking or using water taxis. Access to the island is via Robert Moses Causeway on the western end or William Floyd Parkway on the eastern end. There are parking lots for visitors to the national seashore.

Park Activities
Auto Touring
Biking
✓ Boating
✓ Camping
Climbing
✓ Fishing
✓ Hiking
Horseback Riding
✓ Hunting
Snow Skiing
✓ Swimming
✓ Wildlife Viewing

Information is available from three visitor centers. Sailors Haven is in the middle of Fire Island, across the Great South Bay from Sayville, Long Island. The center is reached by ferry and is closed in winter. The Watch Hill Visitor Center is accessed by ferry from Patchogue and is open mid-May to mid-October. At the east end of Fire Island is the Wilderness Visitor Center, accessible by car via William Floyd Parkway. The center is open year-round.

The park's only campground is near the Watch Hill Visitor Center. Campsite reservations are strongly recommended and can be made online at www.watchhillfi.com; reservations are not accepted by phone. Walk-ins are welcome but obtaining a site is not guaranteed.

Watch Hill: open May to October, 26 tent sites, $25 per night (two-night minimum), water, grills, showers, bathrooms. A marina, snack bar, restaurant, and swimming beach are nearby.

North Carolina

1   Blue Ridge Parkway
2   Cape Hatteras National Seashore
3   Cape Lookout National Seashore
4   Great Smoky Mountains National Park, see Tennessee

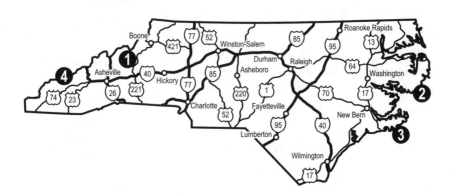

Blue Ridge Parkway

199 Hemphill Knob Rd
Asheville, NC 28803
Phone: 828-298-0398

Blue Ridge Parkway meanders 469 miles between Shenandoah National Park in Virginia and Great Smoky Mountains National Park in North Carolina. The parkway was established in 1936 and encompasses 88,734 acres. It is included in the National Scenic Byways Program as an All-American Road. No entrance fee is charged.

Park Activities
✓ Auto Touring
✓ Biking
✓ Boating
✓ Camping
Climbing
✓ Fishing
✓ Hiking
✓ Horseback Riding
Hunting
✓ Snow Skiing
Swimming
✓ Wildlife Viewing

The parkway is marked every mile by concrete mileposts beginning at MP 0 near Shenandoah National Park and ending at MP 469 at Great Smoky Mountains National Park. Knowing this will help in locating visitor centers and campgrounds.

There are 14 visitor centers along the parkway. All are generally open from May through October. Visitor centers can be found at the following mileposts: Humpback Rocks, MP 5.8; James River, MP 63.8; Peaks of Otter, MP 86.0; Virginia's Explore Park, MP 115; Rocky Knob, MP 169.0; Blue Ridge Music Center, MP 213; Moses H. Cone Memorial Park, MP 294.1; Linn Cove Viaduct, MP 305; Linville Falls, MP 316.4; Mineral Museum, MP 331; Craggy Gardens, MP 364.6; Folk Art Center, MP 382; Visitor Destination Center, MP 384; Waterrock Knob, MP 451.2.

There are nine campgrounds along the parkway. They are listed in milepost order; the first listed is near the beginning of the parkway in Virginia. Limited backcountry camping is available at Basin Cove in Doughton Park and Rock Castle Gorge in Rocky Knob District. Permits are required and must be requested in advance.

Campgrounds in Virginia

Otter Creek: at MP 60.9, open May to October, 45 tent sites, 24 RV sites, $16 per night, drinking water, restrooms, picnic tables, fireplace, dump station, telephone, self-guiding trail, fishing, 21 day maximum stay in summer, 30-foot RV length limit.

Peaks of Otter: at MP 86.0, open May to October, 82 tent sites, 59 RV sites, $16 per night, drinking water, restrooms, picnic tables, fireplace, dump station, camping supplies, telephone, self-guiding trails, fishing, 21 day maximum stay in summer, 30-foot RV length limit. Reservations accepted; call 877-444-6777.

Roanoke Mountain: at MP 120.5, open May to October, 74 tent sites, 30 RV sites, $16 per night, drinking water, restrooms, picnic tables, fireplace, dump station, telephone, 21 day stay limit in summer, 30-foot RV length limit.

Rocky Knob: at MP 167.1, open May to October, 81 tent sites, 28 RV sites, $16 per night, drinking water, restrooms, picnic tables, fireplace, dump station, telephone, nature trails, fishing, 21 day maximum stay in summer, 30-foot RV length limit. Reservations accepted; call 877-444-6777.

Campgrounds in North Carolina

Doughton Park: at MP 239.0, open May to October, 110 tent sites, 25 RV sites, $16 per night, drinking water, restrooms, picnic tables, fireplace, dump station, camping supplies, telephone, fishing, 21 day maximum stay in summer, 30-foot RV length limit. Reservations accepted; call 877-444-6777.

Julian Price Memorial Park: at MP 297.1, open May to October, 129 tent sites, 68 RV sites, $16 per night, drinking water, restrooms, picnic tables, fireplace, dump station, telephone, fishing, 21 day maximum stay in summer, 30-foot RV length limit. Reservations accepted; call 877-444-6777.

Linville Falls: at MP 316.3, open May to October, 50 tent sites, 20 RV sites, $16 per night, drinking water, restrooms, picnic tables, fireplace, dump station, nature trails, fishing, 21 day stay limit in summer, 30-foot RV length limit. Reservations accepted; call 877-444-6777.

Crabtree Meadows: at MP 339.5, open May to October, 71 tent sites, 22 RV sites, $16 per night, drinking water, restrooms, picnic tables, fireplace, dump station, camping supplies, telephone, 21 day maximum stay in summer, 30-foot RV length limit.

Mount Pisgah: at MP 408.6, open May to October, 70 tent sites, 67 RV sites, $16 per night, drinking water, restrooms, showers, picnic tables, fireplace, dump station, camping supplies, telephone, 21 day maximum stay in summer, 30-foot RV length limit. Reservations accepted; call 877-444-6777.

Cape Hatteras National Seashore

1401 National Park Dr
Manteo, NC 27954
Phone: 252-473-2111

Cape Hatteras National Seashore is in eastern North Carolina. It was established in 1953 and encompasses 30,319 acres. Features include sandy beaches, migratory waterfowl, fishing, and historical points of interest. No entrance fee is charged.

Information is available from three visitor centers. Bodie Island Visitor Center is about seven miles south of Whalebone Junction off NC 12. The center is open year-round. Hatteras Island Visitor Center is near Buxton off NC 12 in the Cape Hatteras Lighthouse. It is open all year. Ocracoke Visitor Center is off NC 12 in Ocracoke and is open year-round. All visitor centers close on Christmas Day.

Park Activities
✓ Auto Touring
✓ Biking
✓ Boating
✓ Camping
Climbing
✓ Fishing
✓ Hiking
Horseback Riding
✓ Hunting
Snow Skiing
✓ Swimming
✓ Wildlife Viewing

There are four campgrounds in the park. Reservations can be made for campsites in Ocracoke Campground by calling 877-444-6777. Sites in all other campgrounds are available on a first-come, first-served basis.

Cape Point: two miles south of Buxton off NC 12 near Cape Hatteras Lighthouse, open June to September, 202 sites, $20 per night, drinking water, cold showers, flush toilets, picnic tables, grills, dump station nearby, 14 day maximum stay.

Frisco: off NC 12 east of Frisco and southwest of Buxton, open April to October, 127 sites, $20 per night, cold showers, flush toilets, drinking water, picnic tables, grills, 14 day maximum stay.

Ocracoke: east of Ocracoke along NC 12, open April to October, 136 sites, $23 per night, cold showers, flush toilets, drinking water, picnic tables, grills, dump station nearby, 14 day maximum stay.

Oregon Inlet: nine miles south of Whalebone Junction along NC 12, open April to October, 120 sites, $20 per night, cold showers, flush toilets, drinking water, picnic tables, grills, dump station nearby, marina nearby, 14 day maximum stay.

Cape Lookout National Seashore

131 Charles St
Harkers Island, NC 28531
Phone: 252-728-2250

Park Activities
Auto Touring
Biking
✓ Boating
✓ Camping
Climbing
✓ Fishing
✓ Hiking
Horseback Riding
✓ Hunting
Snow Skiing
✓ Swimming
✓ Wildlife Viewing

Cape Lookout National Seashore is in eastern North Carolina. The seashore is a 56-mile section of the Outer Banks of North Carolina between Ocracoke Inlet and Beaufort Inlet. It was established in 1966. No entrance fee is charged. Access to the area is by ferry; fees vary.

Information is available from the Harkers Island Visitor Center, which is open daily from 9am to 5pm (closed on December 25 and January 1). Information is also available from the Cape Lookout Lighthouse Keepers' Quarters near Bardens Inlet.

There are no established campgrounds or campsites within the park. Beach camping is permitted on all islands; a free permit is required. Vehicles are allowed only on North and South Core Banks. All vehicles and trailers must remain on the ocean beach or within established areas signed for vehicle use.

There is very little shade or shelter on the islands and no source for supplies. Campers must bring everything they need, including water. All trash must be carried out. Camping is limited to 14 consecutive days. Driftwood campfires are permitted below the high tide line. Since this source of wood is extremely limited, cold camping with a self-contained stove is recommended.

North Dakota

1   Theodore Roosevelt National Park

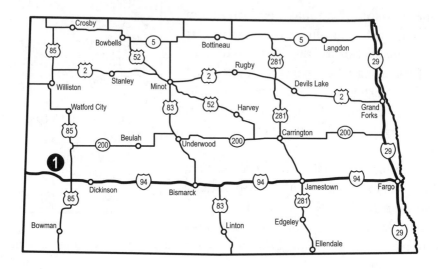

Theodore Roosevelt National Park

PO Box 7
Medora, ND 58645
Phone: 701-623-4466 or 701-842-2333

Park Activities
✓ Auto Touring
✓ Biking
✓ Boating
✓ Camping
Climbing
✓ Fishing
✓ Hiking
✓ Horseback Riding
Hunting
Snow Skiing
Swimming
✓ Wildlife Viewing

Theodore Roosevelt National Park is in southwest North Dakota about 135 miles west of Bismarck. Established in 1947, the 70,447-acre park features scenic badlands along the Little Missouri River and part of Theodore Roosevelt's Elkhorn Ranch. An entrance fee of $10 per vehicle is charged.

Information is available from three visitor centers. Medora Visitor Center is located near Medora at the entrance to the South Unit off I-94. A museum features exhibits of Theodore Roosevelt, area ranching history, and natural history. The North Unit Visitor Center is just west of US 85 about 54 miles north of Belfield. Painted Canyon Visitor Center is off I-94 at Exit #32 in the South Unit.

There are two campgrounds within the park. Campsites are available on a first-come, first-served basis; reservations are not accepted.

Cottonwood: located in the South Unit about six miles from the park entrance, open all year, 76 sites (some pull-thru), $10 per night May through September and $5 per night October through April, picnic tables, fire grills, flush toilets, drinking water, amphitheater, 14 day maximum stay. Limited facilities in winter.

Juniper: located in the North Unit of the park six miles from park entrance, open all year, 50 sites (some pull-thru), $10 per night May through September, $5 October through April, picnic tables, fire grills, flush toilets, drinking water, dump station, 14 day maximum stay. Limited facilities in winter.

Oklahoma

1   Chickasaw National Recreation Area

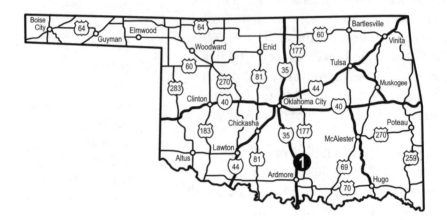

Chickasaw National Recreation Area

1008 W Second St
Sulphur, OK 73086
Phone: 580-622-7234

Chickasaw National Recreation Area is in south-central Oklahoma about 80 miles south of Oklahoma City. The recreation area was originally established as Sulphur Springs Reservation in 1906 and later renamed and redesignated in 1976. The park encompasses nearly 10,000 acres of springs, streams, and lakes. No entrance fee is charged.

Information is available from the park headquarters in Sulphur off US 177 and from the Travertine Nature Center. The latter is open all year except on Thanksgiving Day, Christmas Day, and New Year's Day. Daily activities are scheduled throughout the summer including nature walks and campfire programs.

There are five campgrounds within the park. Reservations are accepted for some sites; call 877-444-6777.

Park Activities
✓ Auto Touring
✓ Biking
✓ Boating
✓ Camping
Climbing
✓ Fishing
✓ Hiking
✓ Horseback Riding
✓ Hunting
Snow Skiing
✓ Swimming
✓ Wildlife Viewing

> **Buckhorn**: nine miles south of Sulphur via US 177 and Buckhorn Road. Campsites situated within four loops. Camping in all loops is limited to 14 days. Boat ramp, picnic area, and dump station nearby.
>
> Loop A: open May to September, 20 sites, $16 per night, restrooms, showers, water. Reservations not accepted.
>
> Loop B: open early May to early September, 5 RV sites and 20 tent sites, $16 per night, restrooms, showers, water. Reservations not accepted.

Loop C: open mid-March to December, 27 RV/tent sites and 14 tent sites, $16 per night, 17 sites have electric hookups ($22 to $24 per night), restrooms, showers, water, amphitheater, trails. Reservations accepted (877-444-6777).

Loop D: open all year, 37 RV/tent sites and 12 tent sites, $16 per night, 24 sites have electric hookups ($22 to $24 per night), restrooms, showers, water, amphitheater. Reservations not accepted.

Cold Springs: near Sulphur about one-half mile east of US 177, open May to September, 63 sites, $14 per night, restrooms, water, 20-foot RV limit, access to hiking trail, 14 day maximum stay. Reservations not accepted.

Guy Sandy: nine miles southwest of Sulphur via OK 7 and Chickasaw Trail Road, open May to August, 40 sites, $14 per night, vault toilets, water, 14 day maximum stay. Boat ramp and picnic area nearby. Reservations not accepted.

Rock Creek: just southwest of Sulphur via 12th Street and Lindsay Avenue, open all year, 105 campsites, $14 per night, mostly tent-only sites but some accommodate RVs, restrooms, water, 14 day maximum stay. Access to hiking trail nearby. Reservations not accepted.

The Point: located eight miles southwest of Sulphur via OK 7 and Charles Cooper Memorial Road.

Lower Loop: open year-round, 37 sites (9 with electric hookups), $16 to $22 per night, restrooms, showers, drinking water. Reservations not accepted.

Upper Loop: open all year, 21 sites (12 with electric hookups), $16 to $22 per night, restrooms, showers, drinking water, amphitheater. Reservations accepted (877-444-6777).

Oregon

1   Crater Lake National Park

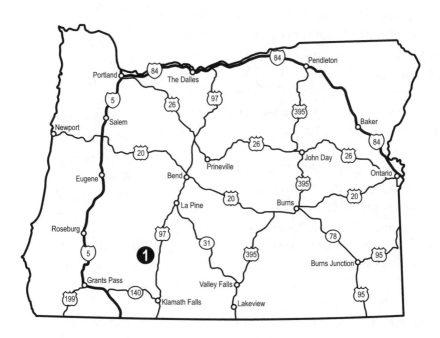

Crater Lake National Park

PO Box 7
Crater Lake, OR 97604
Phone: 541-594-3000

Crater Lake National Park is in southwest Oregon about 75 miles north of Klamath Falls. It was established in 1902 and encompasses 183,244 acres. The lake is the deepest in the United States and is widely known for its intense blue color. An entrance fee of $10 is charged.

Information is available from two visitor centers. Rim Visitor Center is open June through September. A gift shop, cafeteria, and Crater Lake Lodge are nearby. Steel Visitor Center is inside the park headquarters along Rim Drive. A short film and exhibits of the park and its history are available. It remains open all year.

There are two campgrounds within the park. Campsites are available on a first-come, first-served basis. A concessionaire operates Mazama Campground. Backcountry camping is permitted.

Park Activities

✓ Auto Touring
✓ Biking
  Boating
✓ Camping
  Climbing
✓ Fishing
✓ Hiking
  Horseback Riding
  Hunting
  Snow Skiing
  Swimming
✓ Wildlife Viewing

Lost Creek: located in the southeast corner of the park along the spur road to Pinnacles Overlook, open July to October, 16 tent sites, $10 per night, water, flush toilets, picnic tables, fire rings, 14 day stay limit.

Mazama: north of OR 62 about 55 miles northwest of Klamath Falls, open June to September, 212 sites (some with electric hookups), $21 to $29 per night, 50-foot RV length limit, water, flush toilets, dump station, picnic tables, fire rings, coin-operated showers, groceries, gas station, laundry facilities, 14 day maximum stay. Reservations accepted (888-774-2728).

Pennsylvania

1   Delaware Water Gap National Recreation Area

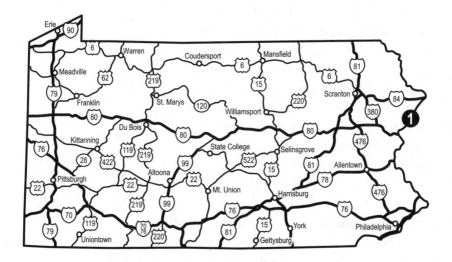

Delaware Water Gap National Recreation Area

1978 River Road
Bushkill, PA 18324
Phone: 570-426-2452

Delaware Water Gap National Recreation
Area is in northeast Pennsylvania about 50
miles east of Scranton. The park preserves
40 miles of the Middle Delaware River
and nearly 70,000 acres of land along
the river's New Jersey and Pennsylvania
shores. It was established in 1965. In
1978, the river was designated a National
Scenic River. No entrance fee is charged
but some areas charge an amenity fee.

Park Activities

✓ Auto Touring
✓ Biking
✓ Boating
✓ Camping
✓ Climbing
✓ Fishing
✓ Hiking
✓ Horseback Riding
✓ Hunting
  Snow Skiing
✓ Swimming
✓ Wildlife Viewing

Information is available from the park
headquarters on River Road in Bushkill, Pennsylvania. It is open
weekdays all year. The Dingmans Falls Visitor Center is open spring
through fall and is located near the junction of US 209 and PA 739.
Kittatinny Point Visitor Center is in New Jersey at I-80 Exit 1; it remains
open daily during summer.

The National Park Service maintains primitive camping areas along the
river for boaters traveling from one access point to another. Length of
stay is limited to one night. Campsites are available on a first-come, first-
served basis. No permit is required and no camping fee is charged.

There is one concession-operated campground at Dingmans Ferry,
Pennsylvania. Camping is also available in the Worthington State Forest
in New Jersey and several private campgrounds nearby.

Dingmans: located in Dingmans Ferry off Route 209, open
mid-January to mid-December, 133 sites, $32 to $37 per night,
restrooms, showers, dump station, playground, camp store.
Reservations accepted; call 570-828-1551 or 877-828-1551. Senior
and Access Passes accepted.

South Carolina

1   Congaree National Park
2   Kings Mountain National Military Park

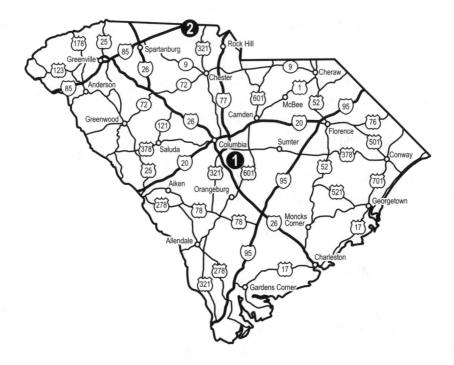

Congaree National Park

100 National Park Road
Hopkins, SC 29061
Phone: 803-776-4396

Congaree National Park is in central South Carolina about 20 miles southeast of Columbia. The park protects the largest contiguous tract of old-growth bottomland hardwood forest remaining in the United States. The 24,600-acre park was established as a National Monument in 1976 and became a National Park in 2003. No entrance fee is charged.

Information is available from the Harry Hampton Visitor Center off Old Bluff Road. It remains open all year between 9am and 5pm (closed on Christmas Day); extended hours on weekends spring to fall. Special programs are offered throughout the year such as guided canoe trips and nature walks.

Park Activities

Auto Touring
Biking
✓ Boating
✓ Camping
Climbing
✓ Fishing
✓ Hiking
Horseback Riding
Hunting
Snow Skiing
Swimming
✓ Wildlife Viewing

Only primitive camping is offered in the park. Over 20 miles of marked hiking trails and 18 miles of marked canoe trails exist within the park. Camping requires a permit, which is available free of charge at the visitor center. Camping is permitted in the wilderness area of the park 200 feet away from backcountry trails and water, and 500 feet away from the visitor center and boardwalk. No facilities are available. Camping is limited to 14 consecutive days. Restrooms are located near the visitor center as is potable water.

Longleaf: located near the park entrance, open all year, eight sites, portable toilets, fire rings with grills, picnic tables. There is no camping fee but a permit is required.

Kings Mountain National Military Park

2625 Park Road
Blacksburg, SC 29702
Phone: 864-936-7921

Kings Mountain National Military Park is in north-central South Carolina about 32 miles northwest of Rock Hill. American frontiersmen defeated the British here on October 7, 1780 at a critical point during the Revolution. The park was established in 1933 and encompasses 3,945 acres. No entrance fee is charged.

Information is available from the visitor center located inside the park along Park Road. The center is open daily 9am to 5pm and from 9am to 6pm weekends between Memorial Day and Labor Day. It is closed on Thanksgiving Day, Christmas Day, and New Year's Day. Features include an educational film and museum exhibit area.

Park Activities
Auto Touring
Biking
Boating
✓ Camping
Climbing
Fishing
✓ Hiking
✓ Horseback Riding
Hunting
Snow Skiing
Swimming
Wildlife Viewing

There is one designated backcountry campsite within the park. The campsite is a three-mile hike from the visitor center and accommodates 10 to 12 people. No advanced registration is required; you can register the day you will be camping. Kings Mountain State Park is adjacent to the military park and has 115 sites with hookups for $16 to $18 per night. Ten tent-only sites ($12-$13 per night) are also available.

South Dakota

1   Badlands National Park
2   Wind Cave National Park

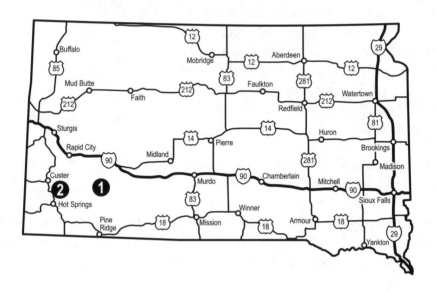

Badlands National Park

PO Box 6
Interior, SD 57750
Phone: 605-433-5361

Badlands National Park is in southwest South Dakota about 80 miles southeast of Rapid City. The park was established in 1929 and consists of 244,000 acres of sharply eroded buttes, pinnacles, and spires blended with the largest, protected mixed-grass prairie in the United States. An entrance fee of $15 is charged.

Park Activities
✓ Auto Touring
✓ Biking
✓ Boating
✓ Camping
Climbing
Fishing
✓ Hiking
✓ Horseback Riding
Hunting
Snow Skiing
Swimming
✓ Wildlife Viewing

Information is available from the Ben Reifel Visitor Center located eight miles south of I-90 Exit 131. The center is open all year and features exhibits of fossils, cultural history, and prairie ecology. Information is also available in summer at the White River Visitor Center on Highway 27 in the Pine Ridge Indian Reservation.

There are two campgrounds within the park. Campsites are available on a first-come, first-served basis. Lodging is available at Cedar Pass Lodge and Badlands Inn.

Cedar Pass: located near the visitor center off SD 240, open all year, 96 sites, $16 per night or $28 per night for sites with electric hookups, limited facilities in winter, flush toilets, dump station (fee charged), 14 day stay limit, no campfires allowed.

Sage Creek: primitive campground 30 miles northwest of visitor center via SD 240 and Sage Creek Rim Road, open all year, 15 sites, no camping fee, pit toilets, no water, no campfires allowed, 14 day stay limit. Horseback riders frequently use the campground. A high-clearance vehicle is required to travel Sage Creek Rim Road.

Wind Cave National Park

26611 US Hwy 385
Hot Springs, SD 57747
Phone: 605-745-4600

Wind Cave National Park is in southwest South Dakota about 50 miles south of Rapid City. The park was established in 1903 and features one of the world's longest and most complex caves and 28,295 acres of mixed-grass prairie and ponderosa pine forest. No entrance fee is charged but there are fees for cave tours ($7 to $23).

Information is available from the Wind Cave Visitor Center located off US 385 about ten miles north of Hot Springs. The center is open all year except on Thanksgiving Day, Christmas Day, and New Year's Day. All cave tours depart from the visitor center. Exhibits feature cave exploration, formations, and history.

Park Activities
✓ Auto Touring
✓ Biking
Boating
✓ Camping
Climbing
Fishing
✓ Hiking
✓ Horseback Riding
Hunting
Snow Skiing
Swimming
✓ Wildlife Viewing

There is one developed campground in the park. Campsites are available on a first-come, first-served basis; no reservations are accepted. Backcountry camping is allowed; a free permit is required.

Elk Mountain: ten miles north of Hot Springs off US 385, open all year, 75 sites (25 pull-thru), $12 per night in warmer months, $6 per night otherwise, limited off-season facilities, flush toilets, drinking water, amphitheater, picnic tables, fire grates, nature trail, 14 day maximum stay. Pets permitted.

Tennessee

1   Big South Fork National River & Recreation Area
2   Cumberland Gap National Historical Park, see Kentucky
3   Great Smoky Mountains National Park
4   Natchez Trace Parkway, see Mississippi
5   Obed Wild & Scenic River

Big South Fork National River & Recreation Area

4564 Leatherwood Rd
Oneida, TN 37841
Phone: 423-286-7275

Big South Fork National River and Recreation Area is in northeast Tennessee and southern Kentucky. The park was established in 1974 and encompasses 125,242 acres. It preserves 90 miles of the Big South Fork of the Cumberland River. No entrance fee is charged.

Information is available from two visitor centers. Bandy Creek Visitor Center is 15 miles west of Oneida, Tennessee, off TN 297. It remains open all year except on Christmas Day. Stearns Depot Visitor Center is south of Whitley City, Kentucky, on KY 92, west of US 27. It is open daily from April through October.

Park Activities
Auto Touring
✓ Biking
✓ Boating
✓ Camping
✓ Climbing
✓ Fishing
✓ Hiking
✓ Horseback Riding
✓ Hunting
Snow Skiing
✓ Swimming
✓ Wildlife Viewing

There are three campgrounds within the park. Backcountry camping is permitted; a $5 to $25 fee is collected depending on group size. Rustic backcountry cabins are available at Charit Creek Lodge. In addition to the campgrounds listed below, there are two developed equestrian campgrounds operated by concessionaires.

Alum Ford: in Kentucky 16 miles northwest of Whitley City via US 27 and KY 700, open all year, six primitive campsites, $5 per night, fire rings, picnic tables, pit toilets, no drinking water, canoe and boat launch nearby, access to hiking trail, 14 day maximum stay. Reservations not accepted; sites are available only on a first-come, first-served basis.

Bandy Creek: 15 miles west of Oneida off TN 297 near visitor center, open all year, 96 sites with water and electric hookups ($22 per night), 49 tent sites ($19 per night), picnic tables, fire rings, restrooms, showers, dump station, swimming pool, 14 day stay limit. Reservations accepted April through October (877-444-6777).

Blue Heron: located on KY 742 west of Stearns in Kentucky, open April through November, 45 sites with water and electric hookups, $17 per night, picnic tables, fire rings, restrooms, showers, dump station, reservations accepted (877-444-6777), 14 day maximum stay.

Great Smoky Mountains National Park

107 Park Headquarters Rd
Gatlinburg, TN 37738
Phone: 865-436-1200

Great Smoky Mountains National Park is in eastern Tennessee and western North Carolina. The park was established in 1934 and encompasses 521,621 acres. No entrance fee is charged.

Information is available from several visitor centers. Cades Cove Visitor Center is near the midpoint of Cades Cove Loop Road. It is open year-round and features a variety of exhibits. Oconaluftee Visitor Center is two miles north of Cherokee, North Carolina, on US 441. It is open all year. An open-air museum is adjacent to the center. Sugarlands Visitor Center is two miles south of Gatlinburg, Tennessee, on US 441. It is open all year and features a 20-minute film and natural history exhibits.

Park Activities
✓ Auto Touring
✓ Biking
Boating
✓ Camping
Climbing
✓ Fishing
✓ Hiking
✓ Horseback Riding
Hunting
Snow Skiing
Swimming
✓ Wildlife Viewing

There are ten developed campgrounds within Great Smoky Mountains National Park. Backcountry camping is allowed in designated sites but a permit, available free, is required. Lodging is available at Le Conte Lodge, which is reached only by a hiking trail. Reservations are required and often must be made one year in advance. Call 865-429-5704 for more information.

Campgrounds in Tennessee

Abrams Creek: six miles north of Chilhowee off US 129, open May to October, 16 sites, $14 per night, 12-foot RV length limit, picnic tables, fire rings, restrooms, running water, seven day maximum stay in summer and fall, 14 day maximum stay rest of year.

Cades Cove: on Cades Cove Road, open year-round, 159 sites, $17 to $20 per night, 40-foot RV length limit (trailers, 35 feet), reservations accepted (877-444-6777), picnic tables, fire rings, restrooms, running water, campstore, dump station, seven day maximum stay summer and fall, 14 day maximum stay rest of year.

Cosby: two miles south of Cosby off US 321, open April to October, 165 sites, $14 per night, 25-foot RV length limit, reservations accepted (877-444-6777), picnic tables, fire rings, restrooms, running water, dump station, seven day maximum stay summer and fall, 14 day stay limit rest of year.

Elkmont: eight miles southwest of Gatlinburg via Little River Road, open March to November, 220 sites, $17 to $23 per night, 32-foot length limit for trailers, 35-foot limit for motor homes, reservations accepted (877-444-6777), picnic tables, fire rings, restrooms, running water, seven day maximum stay summer and fall, 14 days rest of year.

Look Rock: off Foothills Parkway between Walland and Chilhowee, open May to October, 68 sites, $14 per night, no RV length limit, picnic tables, fire rings, restrooms, dump station, running water, seven day maximum stay.

Campgrounds in North Carolina

Balsam Mountain: on Balsam Mountain Road northeast of Cherokee via US 19 and Blue Ridge Parkway, open May to October, 46 sites, $14 per night, 30-foot RV length limit, picnic tables, fire rings, restrooms, running water, seven day maximum stay.

Big Creek: near Waterville south of I-40 Exit #451, open April to October, 12 tent sites, $14 per night, picnic tables, fire rings, restrooms, running water, seven day maximum stay.

Cataloochee: near Maggie Valley about ten miles west of I-40 Exit #20 via US 276 and NC 1395, open March to October, 27 sites, $20 per night, 31-foot RV length limit, reservations required (877-444-6777), picnic tables, fire rings, restrooms, running water, seven day maximum stay summer and fall, 14 day stay limit rest of year.

Deep Creek: three miles north of Bryson City via Deep Creek Road, open April to October, 92 sites, $17 per night, 26-foot RV length limit, picnic tables, fire rings, restrooms, dump station, running water, seven day stay limit summer and fall, 14 days rest of year.

Smokemont: six miles north of Cherokee via Newfound Gap Road, open year-round, 142 sites, $17 to $20 per night, 35-foot length limit for trailers, 40-foot limit for motor homes, reservations accepted (877-444-6777), picnic tables, fire rings, restrooms, running water, dump station, seven day maximum stay summer and fall, 14 day stay limit rest of year.

Obed Wild & Scenic River

PO Box 429
Wartburg, TN 37887
Phone: 423-346-6294

Obed Wild and Scenic River is in eastern Tennessee about 50 miles west of Knoxville. It includes parts of the Obed River, Clear Creek, Daddy's Creek, and Emory River. Over 45 miles of creeks and rivers are included in the wild and scenic river area. It was established in 1976. There is no entrance fee.

Park Activities
Auto Touring
Biking
✓ Boating
✓ Camping
✓ Climbing
✓ Fishing
✓ Hiking
Horseback Riding
✓ Hunting
Snow Skiing
✓ Swimming
✓ Wildlife Viewing

Information is available from the visitor center in Wartburg at 208 North Maiden Street. The center is open all year between 9am and 5pm excluding major holidays. Features include exhibits about the river and a small book store.

There is one primitive campground within the park. Camping is also available in nearby Frozen Head State Natural Area, which has 20 sites for about $13 per night.

Rock Creek: about five miles southwest of Wartburg via Catoosa Road, 11 tent sites, no water or electricity, $7 per night, pit toilets, picnic tables, fire rings. Campsites are available on a first-come, first-served basis.

Texas

1 Amistad National Recreation Area
2 Big Bend National Park
3 Big Thicket National Preserve
4 Guadalupe Mountains National Park
5 Lake Meredith National Recreation Area
6 Padre Island National Seashore

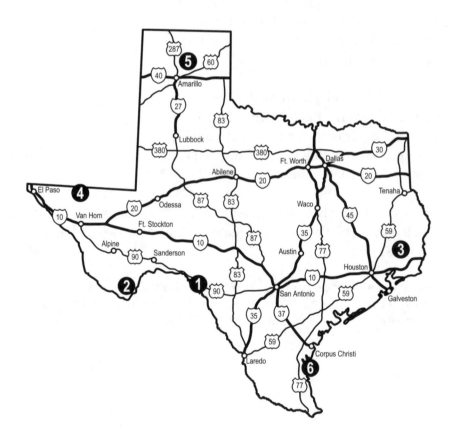

Amistad National Recreation Area

4121 Veterans Blvd
Del Rio, TX 78840
Phone: 830-775-7491

Amistad National Recreation Area is in southwest Texas about 150 miles west of San Antonio. The park consists of 57,292 acres, most of which is under water. It was established in 1965 and became a national recreation area in 1990. No entrance fee is charged but activity fees are charged for boating, hunting, and camping.

Park Activities

Auto Touring
Biking
✓ Boating
✓ Camping
Climbing
✓ Fishing
Hiking
Horseback Riding
✓ Hunting
Snow Skiing
✓ Swimming
✓ Wildlife Viewing

Information is available from the Amistad Visitor Information Center on US 90, northwest of Del Rio. The information center is open all year except Christmas Day. Exhibits relate the story of the dam's construction and describe the natural and cultural resources surrounding the reservoir. Several movies can be viewed in the theater. The Big Bend Natural History Association operates a book store inside the visitor center.

The National Park Service manages five campgrounds in the recreation area. All sites are available on a first-come, first-served basis and may not be reserved. There are no RV hookups at any campground. An RV dump station is located at the Diablo East entrance road.

277 North: off US 277 about ten miles north of Del Rio, open all year, 17 sites, $4 per night, picnic tables, grills, vault toilets, no drinking water, no RV length limit, 14 day maximum stay.

Governors Landing: off US 90 about 12 miles west of Del Rio, open all year, 15 sites, $8 per night, picnic tables, grills, vault toilets, potable water, 28-foot RV length limit, 14 day maximum stay.

Rough Canyon: located 14 miles north of Del Rio and seven miles west of US 277, open all year, four sites, $4 per night, picnic tables, grills, flush toilets and wash water (no hot water), showers available at nearby marina (fee), 14 day stay limit.

San Pedro: off US 90 about seven miles west of Del Rio, open all year, 35 RV/tent sites and 5 tent-only sites, $4 per night, picnic tables, grills, vault toilets, no water, boat ramp nearby, no RV length limit, 14 day stay limit.

Spur 406: about 28 miles northwest of Del Rio via US 90 and TX 406, open all year, eight sites, $4 per night, picnic tables, grills, vault toilets, no drinking water, no RV length limit, 14 day maximum stay.

Big Bend National Park

PO Box 129
Big Bend National Park, TX 79834
Phone: 432-477-2251

Big Bend National Park is in west Texas about 40 miles south of Marathon. The 801,163-acre park was established in 1944 and is one of the largest and least visited national parks in America. Features include mountains, desert, and deep canyons carved by the Rio Grande River. An entrance fee of $20 is charged.

> ## Park Activities
>
> Auto Touring
> Biking
> ✓ Boating
> ✓ Camping
> Climbing
> ✓ Fishing
> ✓ Hiking
> Horseback Riding
> Hunting
> Snow Skiing
> Swimming
> ✓ Wildlife Viewing

Information is available from five visitor centers. Chisos Basin Visitor Center is open all year and is six miles south of Basin Junction. The road is not recommended for RVs over 24 feet because of sharp curves and steep grades. Persimmon Gap Visitor Center (open November to April) is located at the park's northern entrance off US 385. Panther Junction Visitor Center is 26 miles from the north entrance and is open all year. Rio Grande Village Visitor Center is about 20 miles southeast of the Panther Junction Visitor Center and is open November to April. The Castolon Visitor Center is near the Cottonwood Campground and is open November to April.

There are four campgrounds within Big Bend National Park. Primitive camping is available in over 70 campsites that line the park's dirt roads. Backpackers have access to 42 designated backcountry campsites; a backcounty permit is required.

Chisos Basin: six miles south of Basin Junction, open all year, 60 sites, $14 per night, flush toilets, dump station, running water, grills, picnic tables, nature and hiking trails, 14 day stay limit. Due to the narrow and winding road to Chisos Basin and small campsites, trailers over 20 feet and RVs over 24 feet are not recommended. A lodge and grocery store are nearby. Reservations accepted for some sites; call 877-444-6777.

Cottonwood: 22 miles south of Santa Elena Junction off Ross Maxwell Scenic Drive, open all year, 31 sites, $14 per night, pit toilets, picnic tables, grills, drinking water, 14 day maximum stay, 30-foot RV length limit, groceries nearby. The use of generators is prohibited.

Rio Grande Village: about 20 miles southeast of Panther Junction, open all year, 100 sites, some pull-thrus, $14 per night, flush toilets, dump station nearby, running water, picnic tables, grills, laundry and showers nearby, 14 day maximum stay. Reservations accepted for some sites; call 877-444-6777.

Rio Grande Village RV Park: concession-operated campground near the National Park Service's Rio Grande Village campground, open all year, 25 RV sites with full hookups, $33 per night, restrooms, showers, picnic tables, laundry facilities, 14 day maximum stay. Full hookup capability is required. Reservations accepted; call 877-386-4383 or 432-477-2293.

Big Thicket National Preserve

6102 FM 420
Kountze, TX 77625
Phone: 409-951-6700

Big Thicket National Preserve is in eastern Texas. It consists of nine land units and six water corridors encompassing more than 97,000 acres. It was established in 1974 to preserve the rich biological diversity of the area. No entrance fee is charged.

Information is available from the Big Thicket Visitor Center on Farm-to-Market Road 420, about seven miles north of Kountze off US 69. The visitor center is open all year except on Thanksgiving, Christmas, and New Year's Day. It features exhibits, a theater, restrooms, pull-thru parking for large vehicles, picnic tables, and book sales.

There are no developed campgrounds within the park. Visitors come to the preserve to experience backcountry camping. A free permit is required and is available from the visitor center. The permit is valid for ten days. Contact the preserve to obtain a map showing the different units and hiking trails. Several state parks are in the area with developed camping facilities. RV camping is available at the nearby Steinhagen Lake, a Corps of Engineers reservoir located east of Woodville.

Park Activities

✓ Auto Touring
✓ Biking
✓ Boating
✓ Camping
  Climbing
✓ Fishing
✓ Hiking
✓ Horseback Riding
✓ Hunting
  Snow Skiing
✓ Swimming
✓ Wildlife Viewing

Guadalupe Mountains National Park

400 Pine Canyon Rd
Salt Flat, TX 79847
Phone: 915-828-3251

Guadalupe Mountains National Park is located in western Texas about 110 miles east of El Paso. The park was established in 1972 and encompasses over 86,000 acres of mountains and canyons. It contains the highest point in Texas, Guadalupe Peak, at 8,749 feet. An entrance fee of $5 per person is charged.

Information is available from the visitor center located just inside the park off US 62/180. The visitor center is open year-round except Christmas Day. It features extensive natural history exhibits on the park fauna, flora, and geology and a short video. Information is also available from a ranger station in Dog Canyon, which is 65 miles south of Carlsbad, New Mexico, via NM 137.

Park Activities
Auto Touring
Biking
Boating
✓ Camping
Climbing
Fishing
✓ Hiking
✓ Horseback Riding
Hunting
Snow Skiing
Swimming
✓ Wildlife Viewing

There are two developed and ten backcountry campgrounds within the park. Campsites are available on a first-come, first-served basis; no reservations accepted. Backcountry camping requires a free permit that is obtained from the visitor center or Dog Canyon Ranger Station. Over 80 miles of established trails exist within Guadalupe Mountains National Park. Water is available at trailheads only; none in the backcountry.

Dog Canyon: at the park's northern entrance 65 miles south of Carlsbad via NM 137, open all year, four RV sites (no hookups, no dump station), nine tent sites, $8 per night, restrooms, drinking water, 14 day stay limit. Charcoal and wood fires are not permitted.

Pine Springs: located near the visitor center off US 62/180, open all year, 19 RV sites (no hookups, no dump station) and 20 tent sites, $8 per night, drinking water, restrooms, public phone, 14 day maximum stay. Charcoal and wood fires are not permitted.

The following is a list of the ten backcountry campgrounds and the number of sites available. Contact the park for trail information and location of these campgrounds.

Name	Sites
Blue Ridge	5
Bush Mountain	5
Guadalupe Peak	5
Marcus	5
McKittrick Ridge	8
Mescalero	8
Pine Top	8
Shumard	5
Tejas	5
Wilderness Ridge	5

Lake Meredith National Recreation Area

PO Box 1460
Fritch, TX 79036
Phone: 806-857-3151

Lake Meredith National Recreation Area is in northern Texas about 40 miles north of Amarillo. Construction of Sanford Dam on the Canadian River created the lake. It was established in 1965 and encompasses 50,000 acres. No entrance fee is charged.

Information is available from the park headquarters at 419 East Broadway in Fritch. The office is open year-round from 8:00am to 4:30pm, Monday through Friday. The office is also open on Saturdays in summer.

Park Activities

Auto Touring
Biking
✓ Boating
✓ Camping
Climbing
✓ Fishing
✓ Hiking
✓ Horseback Riding
✓ Hunting
Snow Skiing
✓ Swimming
✓ Wildlife Viewing

There are 11 campgrounds within the recreation area. Sites are available on a first-come, first-served basis; reservations are not accepted.

Blue Creek Bridge: on west side of lake about ten miles from Sanford via Highways 3395 and 1913, open all year, no designated campsites, no fee, vault toilets, picnic tables, grills, 14 day maximum stay. This area is one of two designated off-road vehicle use areas. There is no drinking water.

Blue West: on west side of lake about 14 miles from Sanford off Highway 1913, open all year, designated sites, no camping fee, picnic tables, grills, vault toilets, boat ramp nearby, no drinking water, 14 day stay limit.

Bugbee: five miles from Sanford off Highway 3395, open all year, no designated campsites, no camping fee, picnic tables, vault toilets, no drinking water, 14 day maximum stay.

Cedar Canyon: three miles from Sanford off Sanford-Yake Road, open all year, no designated sites, no camping fee, flush toilets (open seasonally), water, boat ramp, dump station nearby, 14 day maximum stay.

Chimney Hollow: on west side of lake near Blue West Campground, open all year, no designated sites, no camping fee, vault toilets, some picnic tables, 14 day stay limit.

Fritch Fortress: four miles north of Fritch via Fritch Drive and El Paso Drive, open all year, individual campsites, no fee, picnic tables, grills, flush toilets (open seasonally), running water, dump station nearby, boat ramp nearby, 14 day maximum stay.

Harbor Bay: two miles west of Fritch via North Holmes Avenue and Lakeview Drive, open all year, no designated campsites, no camping fee, vault toilets, boat ramp, some picnic tables, 14 day stay limit. RV dump station nearby.

McBride Canyon: seven miles south of Fritch on TX 136 and then six miles west, open all year, no designated sites, no camping fee, picnic tables, vault toilets, no water, 14 day maximum stay. Access road can become impassable when wet.

Plum Creek: on west side of lake 24 miles from Sanford south of Highway 1913, open all year, no designated sites, no camping fee, vault toilets, picnic tables, grills, no water, horseback riding trails, hiking and biking, 14 day maximum stay.

Rosita: undeveloped campground located along the Canadian River at the southern end of the park east of US 87/287, open all year, no designated campsites, no fee, no toilets and no water, 14 day maximum stay. This area is designated an off-road vehicle use area.

Sanford-Yake: four miles west of Sanford via Sanford-Yake Road, open all year, individual sites, no fee, picnic tables, flush toilets (open seasonally), running water, grills, dump station nearby, 14 day stay limit, marina and boat ramp nearby.

Padre Island National Seashore

PO Box 181300
Corpus Christi, TX 78480
Phone: 361-949-8068

Padre Island National Seashore is in southern Texas, southeast of Corpus Christi. It was established in 1962 and preserves over 133,000 acres of barrier islands. It is the longest remaining undeveloped barrier island in the world. An entrance fee of $10 is charged.

Information is available from the Malaquite Beach Visitor Center, open daily from 9am to 5pm throughout the year. The visitor center is closed on Christmas Day. Exhibits detail the park's natural history. A small museum displays the island's human and natural history.

Park Activities
✓ Auto Touring
✓ Biking
✓ Boating
✓ Camping
Climbing
✓ Fishing
✓ Hiking
✓ Horseback Riding
Hunting
Snow Skiing
✓ Swimming
✓ Wildlife Viewing

There are five camping areas within the park. Campsites are available on a first-come, first-served basis; reservations are not accepted. A camping permit is required and is available for free at the visitor center or from the Malaquite campground host.

Bird Island Basin: primitive camping on Laguna Madre about four miles northwest of visitor center, open all year, suitable for RVs and tents, $5 per night or purchase an annual pass for $10, chemical toilets, 14 day maximum stay. This area is used primarily for boat launching and windsurfing.

Malaquite: one-half mile from visitor center, open all year, 16 RV sites, 26 RV/tent sites, eight tent-only sites, $8 per night, restrooms, cold showers, picnic tables, dump station, no RV hookups, 14 day stay limit.

North Beach: one-mile stretch of beach at the northern end of the park, primitive camping open to RVs and tents, open all year, no designated sites, no camping fee, no facilities, 14 day maximum stay.

South Beach: defined as the 60-mile stretch from the end of Park Road 22 to the southern end of the park, open all year, no designated sites, no fees, no facilities, 14 day maximum stay. The first five miles of beach are usually suitable for two-wheel-drive vehicles. Many RVers stay in this area during winter. The remaining 55 miles require the use of a four-wheel-drive vehicle. In Texas, beaches are considered highways and all vehicles on them must be street-legal and licensed. Check with the visitor center for beach conditions before driving down the island.

Yarborough Pass: primitive camping on Laguna Madre about 15.5 miles south of visitor center, open all year, no facilities, no designated sites, no camping fee, 14 day maximum stay. The camping area is only accessible by four-wheel-drive vehicles.

Utah

1 Arches National Park
2 Bryce Canyon National Park
3 Canyonlands National Park
4 Capitol Reef National Park
5 Cedar Breaks National Monument
6 Dinosaur National Monument, see Colorado
7 Glen Canyon National Recreation Area
8 Hovenweep National Monument
9 Natural Bridges National Monument
10 Zion National Park

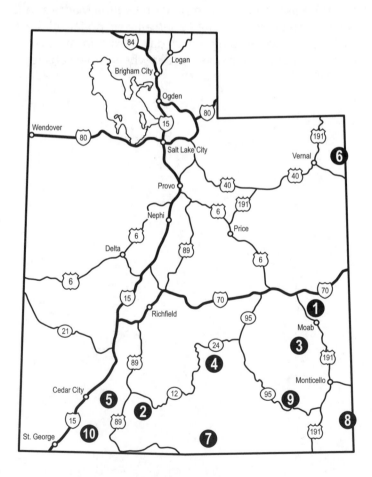

Arches National Park

PO Box 907
Moab, UT 84532
Phone: 435-719-2299

Arches National Park is in southeast Utah five miles north of Moab. Established as a national monument in 1929, the national park now consists of nearly 80,000 acres and 2,000 natural sandstone arches, including the famous Delicate Arch. An entrance fee of $10 is charged.

Information is available from the Arches Visitor Center located along US 191 at the entrance to the park. The visitor center is open daily from 8:00am to 4:30pm with extended hours spring through fall. It closes on Christmas Day. Features include a museum with exhibits on the park's natural and cultural history. A sales area features books, maps, and other publications.

Park Activities

- ✓ Auto Touring
- ✓ Biking
- Boating
- ✓ Camping
- ✓ Climbing
- Fishing
- ✓ Hiking
- Horseback Riding
- Hunting
- Snow Skiing
- Swimming
- ✓ Wildlife Viewing

There is one campground within the park; it usually fills early. Some sites can be reserved by calling 877-444-6777. Wood gathering is prohibited; bring your own wood or charcoal.

Devils Garden: 18 miles north of the park entrance, open all year, 50 sites, $20 per night, flush toilets and water available spring through fall, limited facilities in winter, picnic tables, grills, 30-foot RV length limit, 7 day stay limit.

Bryce Canyon National Park

PO Box 640201
Bryce, UT 84764
Phone: 435-834-5322

Bryce Canyon National Park is in south-central Utah about 70 miles east of Cedar City. Established in 1923, the park encompasses 35,835 acres of colorful and unique rock formations. An entrance fee of $25 is charged.

Information is available from the visitor center along the park road. It remains open year-round except Thanksgiving, Christmas, and New Year's Day. Hours vary by season but are generally 8:00am to 8:00pm. A museum features geology, wildlife, and historic and prehistoric culture exhibits.

Park Activities
✓ Auto Touring
✓ Biking
Boating
✓ Camping
Climbing
Fishing
✓ Hiking
✓ Horseback Riding
Hunting
Snow Skiing
Swimming
✓ Wildlife Viewing

There are two developed campgrounds in the park. Backcountry camping is available at limited sites within the park. A permit is required; cost is $5. Rooms and cabins are available at Bryce Canyon Lodge.

North: located east of the visitor center, open all year, 99 sites, some pull-thrus, $15 per night, reservations accepted (877-444-6777), picnic tables, drinking water, restrooms, dump station (fee charged), 30-foot RV length limit, 14 day maximum stay. Laundry facilities, groceries, and showers nearby.

Sunset: two miles south of visitor center, open spring through fall, 100 sites, $15 per night, picnic tables, drinking water, restrooms, dump station nearby, 45-foot RV length limit, 14 day maximum stay, reservations accepted (877-444-6777).

Canyonlands National Park

2282 SW Resource Blvd
Moab, UT 84532
Phone: 435-719-2313

Canyonlands National Park is located in southeast Utah, southwest of Moab. The park was established in 1964 and consists of 337,570 acres. Among the park's features are prehistoric Indian rock art and ruins. An entrance fee of $10 is charged.

Information is available from two visitor centers. Island in the Sky Visitor Center is in the park's northern area, 32 miles from Moab via US 191 and UT 313. It is open year-round. The Needles Visitor Center is in the southern part of the park and is 76 miles from Moab via US 191 and UT 211. Needles is open daily most of the year; it is closed December to February. Both centers close on Christmas Day and feature exhibits of the area's natural and cultural history.

There are two campgrounds in the park. Campsites are available on a first-come, first-served basis. Primitive backcountry campsites and backpacking zones exist in each district of the park. These sites are accessible by foot, four-wheel-drive vehicle or boat. Permits are required and may be obtained in advance.

> **Park Activities**
>
> ✓ Auto Touring
> ✓ Biking
> ✓ Boating
> ✓ Camping
> ✓ Climbing
>   Fishing
> ✓ Hiking
> ✓ Horseback Riding
>   Hunting
>   Snow Skiing
>   Swimming
>   Wildlife Viewing

Squaw Flat: located in the Needles District west of the visitor center, open all year, 26 sites, $15 per night, restrooms, picnic tables, fire grills, drinking water, 28-foot RV length limit, seven day maximum stay.

Willow Flat: six miles south of Island in the Sky Visitor Center, open all year, 12 sites, $10 per night, picnic tables, fire grills, vault toilets, no drinking water, 28-foot RV length limit, seven day maximum stay.

Capitol Reef National Park

HC 70 Box 15
Torrey, UT 84775
Phone: 435-425-3791 x111

Capitol Reef National Park is in south-central Utah about 130 miles northeast of Cedar City. It was established in 1937 and encompasses 243,559 acres. The park preserves the 100-mile-long Waterpocket Fold, an uplift of sandstone cliffs. There is an entrance fee of $5 per vehicle for traveling the park's scenic drive beyond the Fruita campground.

Information is available from the Capitol Reef Visitor Center located ten miles east of Torrey off UT 24. The center is open year-round, except on Christmas Day. A museum offers an overview of the park's features and exhibits on geology, archeology, and history.

Park Activities

- ✓ Auto Touring
- ✓ Biking
- Boating
- ✓ Camping
- ✓ Climbing
- ✓ Fishing
- ✓ Hiking
- ✓ Horseback Riding
- Hunting
- Snow Skiing
- Swimming
- ✓ Wildlife Viewing

There are three campgrounds in the park. Campsites are available on a first-come, first-served basis. Backcountry camping is allowed; a permit is required and is available free at the visitor center.

Cathedral Valley: 18 miles east of Fremont via UT 72 and Forest Service Road 206, open all year, six sites, no fee, pit toilets, picnic tables, fire grates, no drinking water. A high-clearance, four-wheel-drive vehicle is recommended to reach the campground.

Cedar Mesa: 35 miles south of visitor center via UT 24 and Notom-Bullfrog Road, open all year, five sites, primitive camping, no fee, picnic tables, fire grates, pit toilets, no drinking water.

Fruita: one mile south of visitor center off Scenic Drive, open all year, 71 sites, $10 per night, picnic tables, restrooms with flush toilets, drinking water, dump station, amphitheater, 14 day maximum stay.

Cedar Breaks National Monument

2390 W Hwy 56, Suite 11
Cedar City, UT 84720
Phone: 435-586-9451 or 435-586-0787

Located near Cedar City in southwest Utah, Cedar Breaks National Monument preserves a huge natural amphitheater that has been eroded out of the multicolored Pink Cliffs. The canyon spans some three miles and is over 2,000 feet deep. An entrance fee of $4 per person is charged.

Information is available from the Cedar Breaks Visitor Center on UT 148. The center is open from late May to mid-October. A two-mile hiking trail begins here that will take you to some panoramic overlooks.

Park Activities
✓ Auto Touring
Biking
Boating
✓ Camping
Climbing
Fishing
✓ Hiking
Horseback Riding
Hunting
Snow Skiing
Swimming
✓ Wildlife Viewing

Camping is available in one campground. Reservations can be made for some sites; call 877-444-6777. Campfires are allowed in designated fire pits but campers must provide their own wood.

> **Point Supreme**: about 20 miles east of Cedar City via UT 14 and UT 148, open June to September, 28 sites, $14 per night, 35-foot RV length limit, picnic tables, grills, water, flush toilets, 7 day stay limit. Pets allowed.

Glen Canyon National Recreation Area

PO Box 1507
Page, AZ 86040
Phone: 928-608-6200

Glen Canyon National Recreation Area is
in southern Utah and northern Arizona.
The 1,252,246-acre recreation area was
established in 1972. Lake Powell stretches
186 miles behind Glen Canyon Dam and
is the park's main attraction. An entrance
fee of $15 per vehicle is charged.

Information is available from two visitor
centers. Bullfrog Visitor Center is 86
miles south of Hanksville via UT 95 and
UT 276. The center is open intermittently
beginning in May; call 435-684-7423 for hours. Carl Hayden Visitor
Center is located at Glen Canyon Dam on US 89 in Page, Arizona, and
remains open year-round except winter holidays.

Park Activities

✓ Auto Touring
✓ Biking
✓ Boating
✓ Camping
  Climbing
✓ Fishing
✓ Hiking
  Horseback Riding
  Hunting
  Snow Skiing
✓ Swimming
✓ Wildlife Viewing

In addition to the campgrounds listed below, there are several primitive
camping areas that have no facilities other than pit toilets. These generally
cost $6 to $12 per night. Obtain a map from one of the visitor centers to
locate these. Backcountry camping is also allowed.

Bullfrog RV Park (Painted Hills): concession-operated
campground in Utah about 86 miles south of Hanksville via UT 95
and UT 276, open all year, 24 sites with full hookups, $50 per night,
14 day maximum stay, 50-foot RV length limit, restrooms, showers,
grills, picnic tables. Pets allowed.

Halls Crossing: concession-operated campground in Utah 87
miles west of Blanding via UT 95 and UT 276, open year-round, 24
sites with full hookups, $48 per night, 78 sites without hookups,
restrooms, showers, 14 day maximum stay. Sites can accommodate
RVs up to 60 feet. Pets allowed.

Lees Ferry: National Park Service campground in Arizona five miles north of Marble Canyon off Alternate US 89, open year-round, 54 sites, $12 per night, flush toilets, 35-foot RV length limit, 14 day maximum stay, boat ramp nearby.

Wahweap: concession-operated campground in Arizona four miles north of Glen Canyon Dam off US 89, open all year, 112 tent or self-contained RV sites ($26 per night), 139 full hookup sites ($48 per night), 14 day maximum stay, dump station, showers, laundry, groceries. Marina and boat ramp nearby. Free Wi-Fi is available at the campground but connectivity varies.

Hovenweep National Monument

McElmo Route
Cortez, CO 81321
Phone: 970-562-4282

Hovenweep National Monument is in southeast Utah about 37 miles southeast of Blanding. Established in 1923, the monument preserves a collection of unique prehistoric archeological sites. Some of the sites are in Colorado. A $6 entrance fee per vehicle is charged.

Information is available from the visitor center along Hovenweep Road. The center is open all year and contains exhibits and educational information. There is a small sales area with books about the cultural and natural history of the area.

There is one campground in the park. Campsites are available on a first-come, first-served basis. Some roads to the monument are rough and can become impassable in inclement weather.

> **Hovenweep**: located near the visitor center, open all year, 31 sites, $10 per night, fire rings, picnic tables, flush toilets, running water (5 gallon limit per person), 14 day maximum stay. The campsites are designed for tent camping but a few will accommodate RVs up to 36 feet long. Limited facilities in winter.

Park Activities

Auto Touring
Biking
Boating
✓ Camping
Climbing
Fishing
✓ Hiking
Horseback Riding
Hunting
Snow Skiing
Swimming
Wildlife Viewing

Natural Bridges National Monument

HC 60 Box 1
Lake Powell, UT 84533
Phone: 435-692-1234

Natural Bridges National Monument is in southeast Utah about 40 miles west of Blanding via UT 95 and UT 275. The National Monument was established in 1908 and encompasses 7,636 acres. Features include three natural bridges carved out of sandstone and ancient Indian rock art and ruins. An entrance fee of $6 is charged.

Park Activities
✓ Auto Touring
Biking
Boating
✓ Camping
Climbing
Fishing
✓ Hiking
Horseback Riding
Hunting
Snow Skiing
Swimming
Wildlife Viewing

Information is available from the Natural Bridges Visitor Center at the end of UT 275. The visitor center remains open all year except on winter holidays. An orientation video is shown on request. Exhibits highlight natural and cultural history of the area.

There is one small campground in the monument. Campsites are available on a first-come, first-served basis. Visitors must bring their own wood for campfires; wood gathering is prohibited. Water is available at the visitor center but not at the campground.

Natural Bridges: open all year, 13 sites, $10 per night, picnic tables, fire grates, 26-foot RV length limit, 14 day maximum stay. The campground fills by early afternoon from March through October.

Zion National Park

State Route 9
Springdale, UT 84767
Phone: 435-772-3256

Zion National Park is in southwest Utah about 55 miles south of Cedar City. The park was established in 1919 and encompasses 143,035 acres of colorful canyon and mesa scenery. An entrance fee of $25 per vehicle is charged.

Information is available from two visitor centers. Kolob Canyons Visitor Center is in the northern part of the park east of I-15 at Exit 40. Zion Canyon Visitor Center is near the south entrance to the park along UT 9. Both remain open year-round but close on some winter holidays.

Park Activities

Auto Touring
Biking
Boating
✓ Camping
✓ Climbing
Fishing
✓ Hiking
✓ Horseback Riding
Hunting
✓ Snow Skiing
Swimming
Wildlife Viewing

There are three campgrounds within the park. Backcountry camping is also available; permits required (fee charged).

Lava Point: 25 miles north of the town of Virgin via Kolob Terrace Road, open June through October, six primitive sites, free, pit toilets, water is not available. Vehicles longer than 19 feet are not permitted on the road to the campground. Access roads become impassable when wet.

South: located 1/2 mile from the south entrance, open March through October, 127 sites, $16 per night, flush toilets, dump station, amphitheater, picnic tables, fire grates, running water, 14 day maximum stay. Pets permitted.

Watchman: off UT 9 1/4 mile from the south entrance, open all year, 95 sites with electric hookups ($18-$20 per night), 69 tent-only sites ($16 per night), reservations accepted (877-444-6777), picnic tables, fire grates, running water, flush toilets, dump station, amphitheater, 14 day maximum stay. Pets permitted.

Virgin Islands

1   Virgin Islands National Park

Virgin Islands National Park

1300 Cruz Bay Creek
Saint John, VI 00830
Phone: 340-776-6201 ext. 238

Virgin Islands National Park is on the island of Saint John. Nearly all of Hassel Island in Charlotte Amalie Harbor on Saint Thomas is included as part of the national park. The park was established in 1956 and consists of 12,909 acres. Features include coral reefs, quiet coves, blue-green waters, and white sandy beaches fringed by green hills. No entrance fee is charged but a $4 user fee is collected at Trunk Bay.

Park Activities
Auto Touring
Biking
✓ Boating
✓ Camping
Climbing
✓ Fishing
✓ Hiking
Horseback Riding
Hunting
Snow Skiing
✓ Swimming
Wildlife Viewing

Information is available from the Cruz Bay Visitor Center across from the ferry dock in Cruz Bay. The visitor center is open all year from 8:00am to 4:30pm; it closes on Christmas Day. Maps, brochures, and the latest activity schedule are available from park rangers.

There is one campground in the park. Campground reservations in winter months should be made four to six months in advance by calling 800-539-9998 or 340-776-6330. Backcountry or beach camping is not allowed.

Cinnamon Bay: open all year, bare tent sites ($37 per night), large canvas tents with equipment furnished ($93 per night), screened cottages with propane and electricity ($126 to $163 per night), restrooms, showers, phones, camp store, restaurant. Cottages and canvas tents are equipped with cooking supplies and linens. Rates are lower in the off-season (May through mid-December).

Virginia

1 Assateague Island National Seashore, see Maryland
2 Blue Ridge Parkway, see North Carolina
3 Cumberland Gap National Historical Park, see Kentucky
4 Prince William Forest Park
5 Shenandoah National Park

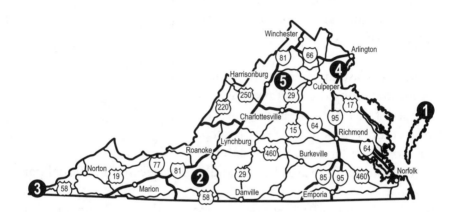

Prince William Forest Park

18100 Park Headquarters Road
Triangle, VA 22172
Phone: 703-221-7181

Prince William Forest Park is in northeast Virginia approximately 30 miles southwest of Arlington. The park was established in 1936 and encompasses over 19,000 acres of pine and hardwood forests. An entrance fee of $5 is charged.

Information is available from the visitor center located along the park road, which is accessed from I-95 at Exit 150. The visitor center is open all year (except winter holidays) and contains exhibits about the history of the area before and after it became a national park.

Park Activities
✓ Auto Touring
✓ Biking
Boating
✓ Camping
Climbing
✓ Fishing
✓ Hiking
Horseback Riding
Hunting
Snow Skiing
Swimming
✓ Wildlife Viewing

There is one National Park Service campground and one operated by a concessionaire. Also available are five cabins built in the 1930s that can accommodate up to 200 people. For information call 703-221-5843.

Oak Ridge: in the western portion of the park off the scenic drive, open year-round, 100 sites, $20 per night, picnic tables, fire grills, drinking water, flush toilets, showers, amphitheater, 14 day maximum stay, 32-foot RV length limit (trailers and fifth-wheels, 26 feet). Reservations accepted; call 877-444-6777.

Prince William Forest RV Campground: concessionaire campground on the north side of the park via VA 234 from I-95 Exit 152, open all year, 72 sites (some full hookups), $31 to $34 per night, hot showers, flush toilets, dump station, laundry facilities, 35-foot RV length limit, 14 day maximum stay. Reservations accepted; call 888-737-5730.

Shenandoah National Park

3655 US Highway 211E
Luray, VA 22835
Phone: 540-999-3500

Shenandoah National Park is in northern
Virginia between Front Royal and
Charlottesville. It was established in 1935
and contains 197,411 acres. Among the
park's features is Skyline Drive, which
winds along the crest of the Blue Ridge
Mountains for 105 miles. An entrance fee
of $15 is charged ($10 December through
February).

Park Activities

✓ Auto Touring
✓ Biking
  Boating
✓ Camping
✓ Climbing
✓ Fishing
✓ Hiking
✓ Horseback Riding
  Hunting
  Snow Skiing
  Swimming
✓ Wildlife Viewing

Information is available from two visitor
centers. Dickey Ridge Visitor Center
is located near Milepost 5 on Skyline Drive (Milepost 0 is at the
northern end of the park). Harry F. Byrd, Sr. Visitor Center is located at
milepost 51 on Skyline Drive. Both visitor centers are open daily except
Thanksgiving Day. Information is also available from the Loft Mountain
Information Center (open weekends only) located at Milepost 79.5 on
Skyline Drive.

There are four campgrounds in Shenandoah National Park. Rental cabins
are available in the Lewis Mountain Campground.

Big Meadows: located at Milepost 51.3, open March to November,
217 campsites, some pull-thrus, $20 per night, reservations
accepted (877-444-6777), picnic tables, grills, amphitheater, coin-
operated showers, laundry facilities, campstore, dump station, 14
day maximum stay.

Lewis Mountain: at Milepost 57.5 on Skyline Drive, open April
to October, 31 sites, $15 per night, picnic tables, grills, showers,
laundry facilities, campstore, cabins available, 30 day stay limit.
Sites are available on a first-come, first-served basis; reservations
are not accepted.

Loft Mountain: at Milepost 79.5 on Skyline Drive, open mid-May through October, 219 sites, some pull-thrus, $15 per night, reservations accepted (877-444-6777), picnic tables, grills, showers, dump station, laundry facilities, campstore, amphitheater, 30 day stay limit.

Mathews Arm: at Milepost 22.1 on Skyline Drive, open mid-May through October, 179 sites, some pull-thrus, $15 per night, reservations accepted (877-444-6777), picnic tables, grills, dump station, 30 day maximum stay, campstore nearby.

Washington

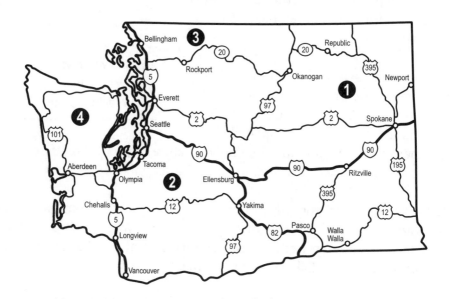

Lake Roosevelt National Recreation Area

1008 Crest Dr
Coulee Dam, WA 99116
Phone: 509-633-9441

Lake Roosevelt National Recreation Area is in northeast Washington between Coulee Dam and Kettle Falls. It was established in 1946 and consists of 100,390 acres. The primary attraction is 130-mile long Franklin D. Roosevelt Lake. There is no entrance fee.

Information is available from the Fort Spokane Museum and Visitor Center located on WA 25, 21 miles north of Davenport. The center is open daily in summer and weekends in September. Features include Fort Spokane, which was converted to an Indian boarding school in 1899.

Park Activities
✓ Auto Touring
Biking
✓ Boating
✓ Camping
Climbing
✓ Fishing
✓ Hiking
Horseback Riding
✓ Hunting
Snow Skiing
✓ Swimming
✓ Wildlife Viewing

There are 27 campgrounds within the recreation area; some are only accessible by boat. Reservations are accepted for campsites in Fort Spokane, Keller Ferry, Kettle Falls, and Spring Canyon. Sites in all other campgrounds are available on a first-come, first-served basis.

Cloverleaf: boat-in or walk-in campground near Gifford, open all year, nine sites, $10 per night May through September, $5 per night rest of year, vault toilets, water, boat dock.

Crystal Cove: boat-in campground on the Spokane River Arm, open all year, three sites, vault toilets, no water, no camping fee.

Detillion: boat-in campground on the Spokane River Arm, open all year, 12 sites, vault toilets, water, boat dock, no camping fee.

Enterprise: boat-in campground between mile 55 and 60, open all year, 13 sites, vault toilets, no water, no camping fee.

Evans: one mile south of Evans along WA 25, open all year, 43 sites, $10 per night May through September, $5 per night rest of year, flush toilets, drinking water, boat ramp, boat dock, dump station, amphitheater, 14 day maximum stay.

Fort Spokane: 21 miles north of Davenport on WA 25, open all year, 67 sites, $10 per night May through September, $5 per night rest of year, flush toilets, drinking water, boat ramp, boat dock, dump station, amphitheater, 14 day maximum stay. Reservations accepted; call 877-444-6777.

Gifford: two miles south of Gifford along WA 25, open all year, 42 sites, $10 per night May through September, $5 per night rest of year, vault toilets, water, boat ramp, boat dock, dump station, 14 day stay limit.

Goldsmith: boat-in campground between mile 15 and 20, open all year, three sites, vault toilets, no water, no camping fee.

Haag Cove: eight miles southwest of Kettle Falls via WA 20 and County Road 3, open all year, 16 sites, $10 per night May through September, $5 per night rest of year, vault toilets, water, boat dock, 14 day stay limit.

Halversen Canyon: boat-in campground, open all year, one site, vault toilets, no water, no camping fee.

Hawk Creek: 13 miles east of Creston via US 2 and Miles Creston Road, open all year, 21 sites, $10 per night May through September, $5 per night rest of year, vault toilets, water, boat ramp and dock, 14 day stay limit.

Hunters: two miles west of Hunters off WA 25, open all year, 39 sites, $10 per night May through September, $5 per night rest of year, flush toilets, water, boat ramp, boat dock, dump station, 14 day stay limit.

Jones Bay: 18 miles north of Wilbur off WA 21, open all year, nine sites, $10 per night May through September, $5 per night rest of year, vault toilets, no drinking water, boat ramp and dock, 14 day stay limit.

Kamloops: seven miles northwest of Kettle Falls via US 395, open all year, 17 sites, $10 per night May through September, $5 per night rest of year, vault toilets, water, boat dock, 14 day maximum stay.

Keller Ferry: 15 miles north of Wilbur via WA 21, open all year, 55 sites, $10 per night May through September, $5 per night rest of year, flush toilets, drinking water, boat ramp, boat dock, marina, dump station, 14 day maximum stay. Reservations accepted; call 877-444-6777.

Kettle Falls: four miles west of Kettle Falls via Old Kettle Road, open year-round, 76 sites, $10 per night May through September, $5 per night rest of year, flush toilets, drinking water, marina, boat ramp, boat dock, dump station, 14 day maximum stay. Reservations accepted; call 877-444-6777.

Kettle River: ten miles north of Kettle Falls via US 395, open all year, 13 sites, $10 per night May through September, $5 per night rest of year, vault toilets, water, boat dock, 14 day maximum stay.

Marcus Island: seven miles north of Kettle Falls via WA 25, open year-round, 27 sites, $10 per night May through September, $5 per night rest of year, vault toilets, water, boat dock and ramp, 14 day stay limit.

North Gorge: 18 miles north of Kettle Falls off WA 25, year-round, 12 sites, $10 per night May through September, $5 per night rest of year, vault toilets, water, boat ramp, boat dock, 14 day maximum stay.

Penix: boat-in campground between mile 20 and 25, open all year, three sites, no camping fee, vault toilets, boat dock, no drinking water.

Plum Point: boat-in campground between mile 5 and 10, open all year, four sites, no fee, vault toilets, boat dock, no water.

Ponderosa: boat-in campground on Spokane River Arm, open year-round, eight sites, vault toilets, no water, no fee.

Porcupine Bay: 18 miles north of Davenport via WA 25 and Porcupine Bay Road, open all year, 31 sites, $10 per night May through September, $5 per night rest of year, flush toilets, water, boat ramp, boat dock, dump station, 14 day maximum stay.

Snag Cove: eight miles northeast of Kamloops Campground via Northport Flat Creek Road, open year-round, nine sites, $10 per night May through September, $5 per night rest of year, vault toilets, water, boat ramp, boat dock, 14 day maximum stay.

Spring Canyon: three miles east of Grand Coulee via WA 174, open all year, 87 sites, $10 per night May through September, $5 per night rest of year, flush toilets, water, boat ramp, boat dock, dump station, 14 day maximum stay. Reservations accepted; call 877-444-6777.

Sterling Point: boat-in campground between mile 30 and 35, open all year, five sites, vault toilets, no fee, no water.

Summer Island: boat-in campground near mile 110, six sites, vault toilets, boat dock, no water, no camping fee.

Mount Rainier National Park

55210 238th Ave E
Ashford, WA 98304
Phone: 360-569-2211

Park Activities

✓ Auto Touring
✓ Biking
  Boating
✓ Camping
✓ Climbing
✓ Fishing
✓ Hiking
✓ Horseback Riding
  Hunting
✓ Snow Skiing
  Swimming
✓ Wildlife Viewing

Mount Rainier National Park is in west-central Washington about one hundred miles southeast of Olympia. The park was established in 1899 and encompasses 235,625 acres. About 97 percent of the park is designated wilderness. An entrance fee of $15 per vehicle is charged.

Information is available from three visitor centers. Jackson Visitor Center is in Paradise off the main park road and is open daily June to October. Features include exhibits of the natural and cultural history of the park. Ohanapecosh Visitor Center is in the southeast corner of the park off WA 123 and is open daily from June to October. The Sunrise Visitor Center is open daily June to September and is located in the northeast corner of the park on Sunrise Park Road.

There are five National Park Service campgrounds. Reservations are strongly recommended for campsites in Cougar Rock and Ohanapecosh between late June and Labor Day. Otherwise, campsites are available on a first-come, first-served basis.

> **Cougar Rock**: southwest corner of park just over two miles north of Longmire, open May to October, 173 sites, $12 to $15 per night, 35-foot RV length limit (27 feet for trailers), water, flush toilets, dump station, fire grates, picnic tables, amphitheater, hiking trails, 14 day maximum stay. Reservations accepted; call 877-444-6777.

> **Ipsut Creek**: in the northwest corner of park five miles east of Carbon River Entrance, open all year, 12 walk-in sites, no camping fee, picnic tables, vault toilets, no potable water, 14 day maximum stay. Fires prohibited.

Mowich Lake: in the northwest corner of park at end of WA 165, open July to October, 10 walk-in sites, vault toilets, no water, no camping fee. Fires prohibited.

Ohanapecosh: 11 miles northeast of Packwood on WA 123 in the southeast corner of park, open May to October, 188 sites, $12 to $15 per night, 32-foot RV length limit (27 feet for trailers), drinking water, flush toilets, dump station, amphitheater, picnic tables, fire grates, hiking trails, 14 day maximum stay. Reservations accepted; call 877-444-6777.

White River: five miles west of White River Entrance off WA 410, open June to September, 112 sites, $12 per night, drinking water, flush toilets, picnic tables, fire grates, amphitheater, 14 day maximum stay.

North Cascades National Park

810 State Route 20
Sedro-Woolley, WA 98284
Phone: 360-854-7200

North Cascades National Park is in
northern Washington about 50 miles east
of Mount Vernon. It was established in
1968 and is 684,242 acres in size. Within
the park are two national recreation
areas: Ross Lake and Lake Chelan. Over
93 percent of the park is included in the
Stephen Mather Wilderness. No entrance
fees are charged.

Information is available from the park
headquarters in Sedro-Woolley on State
Highway 20. Information can also be obtained from two visitor centers.
Golden West Visitor Center is at Stehekin Landing near the north end
of Lake Chelan. There is no road access to Golden West. The North
Cascades Visitor Center is along WA 20 near the town of Newhalem and
is open May through October.

Park Activities
✓ Auto Touring
✓ Biking
✓ Boating
✓ Camping
✓ Climbing
✓ Fishing
✓ Hiking
Horseback Riding
Hunting
Snow Skiing
Swimming
✓ Wildlife Viewing

There are four vehicle-accessible campgrounds within North Cascades
National Park. Most campsites are available on a first-come, first-served
basis. There are more than 200 backcountry campsites, from boat-in
sites to high alpine backpacking sites. All backcountry sites require a
free permit that is issued on a first-come, first-served basis. The vehicle-
accessible campgrounds are described below.

Colonial Creek: ten miles east of Newhalem on WA 20, open
May to October, 142 sites, $12 per night, picnic tables, fire rings,
drinking water, flush toilets, dump station, boat ramp, trails, 14 day
stay limit.

Goodell Creek: one mile west of Newhalem on WA 20, open all
year, 21 sites, no large RVs, $10 per night, picnic tables, fire rings,
vault toilets, drinking water, 14 day maximum stay.

Gorge Lake: located just outside the town of Diablo, open year-round, primitive camp with six sites, vault toilets, no water, no camping fee, 14 day maximum stay.

Hozomeen: at north end of Ross Lake south of Canadian border, open June to October, 75 sites, no camping fee, picnic tables, fire rings, drinking water, vault toilets, 14 day maximum stay. This campground can only be reached by following Silver-Skagit Road, a gravel road, for 40 miles from Hope, British Columbia in Canada.

Newhalem Creek: on WA 20 in Newhalem, open May to September, 111 sites, $12 per night, reservations accepted (877-444-6777), picnic tables, fire rings, drinking water, flush toilets, dump station, 14 day maximum stay. Large RVs can be accommodated.

Olympic National Park

600 E Park Ave
Port Angeles, WA 98362
Phone: 360-565-3130

Olympic National Park is in northwest Washington about 100 miles northwest of Olympia. It was established in 1938 and encompasses 913,339 acres. Among its features are glacier-capped mountains, valleys, meadows, lakes, and miles of beaches. An entrance fee of $15 is charged.

Information is available from three visitor centers. The main visitor center is in Port Angeles at 3002 Mount Angeles Road. It remains open year-round. Hurricane Ridge Visitor Center (open daily in summer) is about 17 miles south of Port Angeles along Heart O' the Hills Road. The Hoh Rain Forest Visitor Center (open daily in summer) is located on Upper Hoh Road about 16 miles east of US 101.

Park Activities

✓ Auto Touring
✓ Biking
✓ Boating
✓ Camping
✓ Climbing
✓ Fishing
✓ Hiking
✓ Horseback Riding
  Hunting
✓ Snow Skiing
✓ Swimming
✓ Wildlife Viewing

The National Park Service maintains 16 campgrounds throughout the park. Campsites are available on a first-come, first-served basis except for sites in Kalaloch, which operates on a reservation system in summer.

Altaire: 13 miles southwest of Port Angeles via US 101 and Olympic Hot Springs Road, open May to September, 30 sites, $12 per night, water, flush toilets, picnic tables, fire pit or grill, 35-foot RV length limit, 14 day stay limit. Campground subject to closure during low visitor use periods.

Deer Park: 22 miles southeast of Port Angeles via US 101 and Deer Park Road, open June to September, 14 tent sites, $10 per night, pit toilets, picnic tables, fire pit or grill, no water, 14 day maximum stay. Campground subject to closure during low visitor use periods.

Dosewallips: 15 miles west of Brinnon on Dosewallips Road, open June to September, 30 walk-in sites, $10 per night, pit toilets, picnic tables, fire pit or grill, nature trails, no water, 14 day maximum stay. Part of access road to campground was washed out in 2002 and remains closed. Campers must hike 5 miles to reach the campground.

Elwha: 12 miles southwest of Port Angeles via US 101 and Olympic Hot Springs Road, open all year, 40 sites, $12 per night, water, restrooms, picnic tables, fire pit or grill, 35-foot RV length limit, 14 day maximum stay. Limited facilities in winter.

Fairholme: 26 miles west of Port Angeles on US 101, open April to October, 88 sites, $12 per night, water, restrooms, dump station, picnic tables, fire pit or grill, boat ramp, restaurant, 21-foot RV length limit, 14 day maximum stay. Campground subject to closure during low visitor use periods.

Graves Creek: 20 miles east of Amanda Park on Quinault River Road, open all year, 30 sites, $12 per night, pit toilets, no water in winter, picnic tables, fire pit or grill, nature trails, 21-foot RV length limit, 14 day maximum stay.

Heart O' the Hills: five miles south of Port Angeles on Heart O' the Hills Road, open all year, 105 sites, $12 per night, water, restrooms, picnic tables, fire pit or grill, nature trails, 35-foot RV length limit, 14 day stay limit.

Hoh: on Hoh River Road near visitor center, open year-round, 88 sites, $12 per night, water, restrooms, dump station, picnic tables, fire pit or grill, 21-foot RV length limit, 14 day maximum stay.

Kalaloch: 35 miles south of Forks on US 101, open all year, 170 sites, $18 per night in summer, $14 per night rest of year, water, flush toilets, dump station, picnic tables, fire pit or grill, 35-foot RV length limit, 14 day maximum stay. Reservations accepted; call 877-444-6777.

Mora: 14 miles west of Forks on Mora Road via WA 110, open all year, 94 sites, some pull-thrus, $12 per night, water, restrooms, dump station, picnic tables, fire pit or grill, 35-foot RV length limit, 14 day maximum stay.

North Fork: 20 miles northeast of Amanda Park via North Shore Road, nine sites, $10 per night, pit toilets, picnic tables, fire pit or grill, no water, 14 day stay limit. Not recommended for larger RVs and trailers. Campground subject to closure during low visitor use periods.

Ozette: 24 miles southwest of Sekiu via WA 112 and Hoko Ozette Road, open all year, 15 sites, $12 per night, water in summer, restrooms nearby, picnic tables, fire pit or grill, nature trails, boat ramp, 21-foot RV length limit, 14 day maximum stay.

Queets: 21 miles east of Queets via US 101 and Queets River Road, 20 sites, $10 per night, open all year, pit toilets, picnic tables, fire pit or grill, no water, 14 day maximum stay. RVs and trailers not recommended. Campground may close in winter.

Sol Duc: 40 miles west of Port Angeles via US 101 and Sol Duc River Road, open all year, 82 sites, $14 per night, water in summer, restrooms, dump station, picnic tables, fire pit or grill, nature trails, 35-foot RV length limit, 14 day maximum stay. Campground subject to closure during low visitor use periods.

South Beach: three miles south of Kalaloch campground along US 101, open May to September, 50 sites, $10 per night, flush toilets, water, picnic tables, fire pit, 35-foot RV length limit, 14 day maximum stay.

Staircase: 16 miles northwest of Hoodsport via WA 119, open year-round, 47 sites, $12 per night, flush toilets, water in summer, picnic tables, fire pit or grill, 35-foot RV length limit, 14 day maximum stay.

West Virginia

1 Chesapeake & Ohio Canal National Historical Park, see Maryland
2 New River Gorge National River

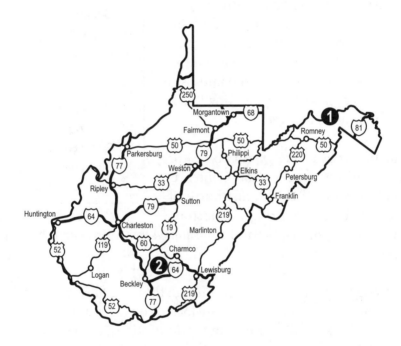

New River Gorge National River

PO Box 246
Glen Jean, WV 25846
Phone: 304-465-0508

New River Gorge National River is in southern West Virginia near Beckley. It was established in 1978 to protect 53 miles of the New River between Hinton and Fayetteville. The park encompasses 70,762 acres of land along the New River. No entrance fee is charged.

Information is available from two visitor centers. Canyon Rim Visitor Center is north of Beckley off US 19, just north of the New River Gorge Bridge. Sandstone Visitor Center is located in Sandstone at I-64 Exit 139. Both remain open year-round.

Park Activities

- ✓ Auto Touring
- ✓ Biking
- ✓ Boating
- ✓ Camping
- ✓ Climbing
- ✓ Fishing
- ✓ Hiking
- ✓ Horseback Riding
- ✓ Hunting
- Snow Skiing
- Swimming
- ✓ Wildlife Viewing

There are seven primitive campgrounds in the park. Sites are available on a first-come, first-served basis. All are located on maintained gravel roads but are usually some distance from service stations, markets, and public phones. All provide easy access to the river for fishing and whitewater boating. Campers are required to register with a park ranger.

Army Camp: about two miles west of Prince off WV 41, open all year, 11 sites, no fee, picnic tables, grills, toilet facilities, no drinking water, 14 day maximum stay. The campground can accommodate self-contained RVs.

Brooklyn: located about ten miles east of Oak Hill, open all year, four walk-in sites, one drive-in site, no fee, no water, 14 day stay limit.

Glade Creek: located at the end of Glade Creek Road off WV 41 near Prince, open all year, six walk-in and five drive-in sites, no fee, picnic tables, grills, toilet facilities, no water, 14 day maximum stay. Campground cannot accommodate large RVs.

Grandview Sandbar: located along Glade Creek Road off WV 41 near Prince, open all year, six walk-in and ten vehicle sites, no fee, picnic tables, grills, toilet facilities, no water, 14 day maximum stay. Not recommended for large RVs.

Stone Cliff: located off County Road 25 near Thurmond, open all year, six walk-in sites and one vehicle site, no fee, no water, no facilities, 14 day maximum stay. The area is subject to flooding.

Thayer: located about 12 miles east of Glen Jean via County Road 25, open all year, no fee, no water, 14 day stay limit.

War Ridge/Backus Mountain: located two miles off WV 41 via Backus Rd and 22/7 Rd, open all year, eight vehicle sites, picnic tables, portable toilets, fire rings, no fee, no water, 14 day maximum stay. Not recommended for large RVs.

Wisconsin

1   Apostle Islands National Lakeshore
2   Saint Croix National Scenic Riverway

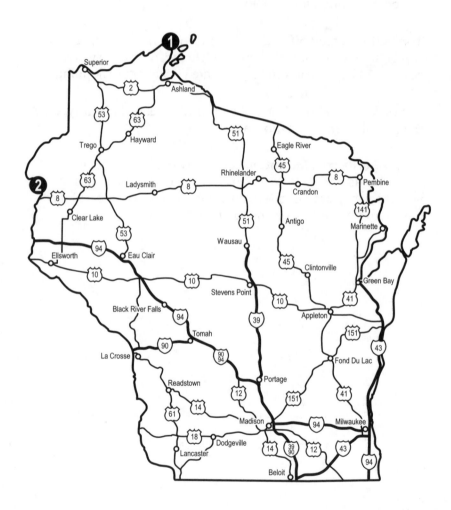

Apostle Islands National Lakeshore

415 Washington Ave
Bayfield, WI 54814
Phone: 715-779-3397

Park Activities

Auto Touring
Biking
✓ Boating
✓ Camping
Climbing
✓ Fishing
✓ Hiking
Horseback Riding
✓ Hunting
Snow Skiing
✓ Swimming
✓ Wildlife Viewing

Apostle Islands National Lakeshore is in northern Wisconsin about 12 miles north of Washburn. The park was established in 1970 and is comprised of 21 islands and 12 miles of mainland Lake Superior shoreline. There is no entrance fee.

Information is available from three visitor centers. Bayfield Visitor Center is in the old Bayfield County Courthouse on Washington Avenue between Fourth and Fifth Streets in Bayfield. Hours vary by season but the visitor center is open year-round. Little Sand Bay Visitor Center is 13 miles north of Bayfield on Little Sand Bay Road and is open in summer. Stockton Island Visitor Center is staffed intermittently but is open daily for self service use in summer.

Only primitive camping is available. No camping areas are accessible by road. A camping permit is required and is valid for 14 days; a fee of $10 per night is charged. There are numerous private and public campgrounds nearby that can accommodate RVers.

Saint Croix National Scenic Riverway

401 N Hamilton St
Saint Croix Falls, WI 54024
Phone: 715-483-2274

Saint Croix National Scenic River is in northwest Wisconsin. It was established in 1968 to preserve 252 miles of the Namekagon and Saint Croix Rivers. There is no entrance fee.

Information is available from two visitor centers. The Saint Croix Visitor Center is located on Hamilton Street in Saint Croix Falls; it remains open year-round. The Namekagon River Visitor Center, located on Highway 63 in Trego, is open only in summer.

Park Activities
Auto Touring
Biking
✓ Boating
✓ Camping
Climbing
✓ Fishing
✓ Hiking
✓ Horseback Riding
✓ Hunting
Snow Skiing
Swimming
✓ Wildlife Viewing

Only primitive camping is available along the riverway, which is divided into four federal camping zones as described below:

North of Nevers Dam: camping is restricted to designated sites and is limited to three nights.

Nevers Dam to Highway 8: camping is restricted to designated sites and is limited to three nights.

Highway 8 to Soo Line High Bridge: camping is restricted to designated sites and is limited to three nights. A free camping permit is required. Toilets are provided only at Eagle's Nest Campground; elsewhere, portable toilets must be packed in and out and used.

Soo Line High Bridge to Stillwater: few disgnated campsites. Camping is only allowed on islands in this zone. There is a seven-night limit.

Wyoming

1   Bighorn Canyon National Recreation Area, see Montana
2   Devils Tower National Monument
3   Grand Teton National Park
4   Yellowstone National Park

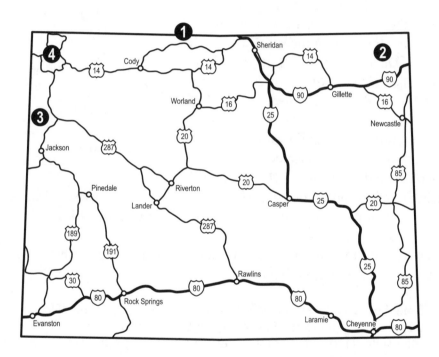

Devils Tower National Monument

PO Box 10
Devils Tower, WY 82714
Phone: 307-467-5283

Devils Tower National Monument is in northeast Wyoming about 27 miles northwest of Sundance. Established in 1906, the 1,346-acre park is the nation's first national monument. The nearly vertical Devils Tower rises 1,267 feet above the Belle Fourche River. An entrance fee of $10 per vehicle is charged.

Information is available from the Devils Tower Visitor Center located at the end of the park road at the base of the Tower. The visitor center is open spring through fall; hours vary by season. Features include exhibits of the natural and cultural history and book sales.

Park Activities
Auto Touring
Biking
Boating
✓ Camping
✓ Climbing
Fishing
✓ Hiking
Horseback Riding
Hunting
Snow Skiing
Swimming
✓ Wildlife Viewing

There is one campground in the monument. Campsites are available on a first-come, first-served basis.

Belle Fourche: located along the park road, open spring to fall, 50 sites, $12 per night, 35-foot RV length limit, picnic tables, flush toilets, drinking water, amphitheater, trails, 14 day maximum stay.

Grand Teton National Park

PO Drawer 170
Moose, WY 83012
Phone: 307-739-3300

Grand Teton National Park is in northwest
Wyoming. It was established in 1929 and
protects nearly 310,000 acres of rugged
mountains and placid lakes. An entrance
fee of $25 per vehicle is charged. The
fee also includes entrance into nearby
Yellowstone National Park. The park
receives over four million visitors each
year, primarily between Memorial Day
and the end of September.

Park Activities
✓ Auto Touring
✓ Biking
✓ Boating
✓ Camping
✓ Climbing
✓ Fishing
✓ Hiking
✓ Horseback Riding
Hunting
Snow Skiing
Swimming
✓ Wildlife Viewing

Information is available from three visitor
centers. Colter Bay Visitor Center is open May to October and is located
adjacent to Jackson Lake about 25 miles north of Moose. Jenny Lake
Visitor Center is about eight miles north of Moose and remains open
May to September. The Craig Thomas Discovery & Visitor Center is
open all year and is 12 miles north of Jackson off US 26.

There are seven campgrounds within Grand Teton National Park. Most
campsites are available on a first-come, first-served basis. Backcountry
camping requires a permit and is limited to designated sites.

Colter Bay: 25 miles north of Moose off US 89, open May to
September, 350 sites, $20.50 per night, flush toilets, dump station,
hot showers, laundry facilities, 14 day stay limit.

Colter Bay RV Park: concession-operated campground off US 89
about 25 miles north of Moose, open May through September, 112
RV sites with full hookups, some pull-thrus, $57 per night, 14 day
stay limit. Reservations accepted; call 800-628-9988.

Flagg Ranch: concession-operated campground north of Jackson Lake (between Grand Teton and Yellowstone National Parks), open June to September, 100 RV sites with full hookups (20 amp service), some pull-thrus, $64 per night, 75 tent sites, $35 per night, showers, laundry facilities, fire pit, picnic tables. Reservations accepted; call 800-443-2311 for more information.

Gros Ventre: ten miles northeast of Jackson via US 26 and Gros Ventre Drive, open May to October, 350 sites, $20.50 per night, flush toilets, dump station, 14 day stay limit. The campground generally fills in the evening, if at all.

Jenny Lake: eight miles north of Moose on Teton Park Road, open May to September, 49 tent sites, $20.50 per night, flush toilets, groceries nearby, boat ramp, hiking trail, 14 day maximum stay. This is the park's most popular campground and is usually full by 11am.

Lizard Creek: at the north end of the park off US 89 about 32 miles north of Moose, open June to September, 60 sites, $20.50 per night, 30-foot RV length limit, flush toilets, 14 day maximum stay. Campground rarely fills.

Signal Mountain: 18 miles north of Moose along Teton Park Road, open May to October, 86 sites, $20.50 per night, 30-foot RV length limit, flush toilets, dump station, groceries nearby, marina nearby, 14 day maximum stay. Campground generally fills by mid-afternoon.

Yellowstone National Park

PO Box 168
Yellowstone National Park, WY 82190
Phone: 307-344-7381

Yellowstone National Park is located in northwest Wyoming; small portions are also in Idaho and Montana. The park was established in 1872 and consists of more than two million acres of mountain scenery, meadows, and lakes. There are more geysers and hot springs here than anywhere in the world. The entrance fee is $25 per vehicle.

Park Activities
✓ Auto Touring
✓ Biking
✓ Boating
✓ Camping
Climbing
✓ Fishing
✓ Hiking
✓ Horseback Riding
Hunting
✓ Snow Skiing
Swimming
✓ Wildlife Viewing

Information is available from five visitor centers and numerous ranger stations. Albright Visitor Center is five miles south of the North Entrance in Mammoth Hot Springs and is open daily year-round. Canyon Visitor Center is open May to October and is located in the Canyon Village area. Fishing Bridge Visitor Center is one mile off the Grand Loop Road on East Entrance Road and is open May to September. Grant Village Visitor Center is open May to September and is on the shore of the West Thumb of Yellowstone Lake in Grant Village. Old Faithful Visitor Center is open April to November and is on Grand Loop Road 16 miles south of Madison Junction.

There are 12 campgrounds within Yellowstone National Park. The National Park Service operates seven of these; five are managed by a concessionaire. Sites managed by the Park Service are available on a first-come, first-served basis. To make reservations for sites in the concession-operated campgrounds, call 866-439-7375. A limited number of sites can accommodate RVs over 30 feet; reservations are recommended.

Bridge Bay: concession-operated campground 18 miles north of West Thumb Junction on Yellowstone Lake, open May to September, 432 sites, $20.50 per night, flush toilets, dump station, amphitheater, groceries nearby, marina and boat ramp nearby, generators permitted, 40-foot RV length limit, 14 day stay limit.

Canyon: concession-operated campground in Canyon Village off Grand Loop Road, open June to September, 273 sites, $25 per night, flush toilets, showers, laundry facilities, amphitheater, restaurant, groceries, service station, dump station, generators permitted, 40-foot RV length limit, 14 day maximum stay.

Fishing Bridge RV Park: concession-operated campground 26 miles west of East Entrance, open May to September, 346 sites with full hookups (50-amp), $45 per night, flush toilets, showers, dump station, laundry, restaurant and groceries nearby, 40-foot RV length limit, no length of stay limit. Campground is designed for hard-sided vehicles only, no tents or canvas vehicles permitted. Discount passes are not honored at this campground.

Grant Village: concession-operated campground 22 miles north of South Entrance on Yellowstone Lake, open June to September, 430 sites, $25 per night, flush toilets, showers, laundry facilities, dump station, groceries nearby, boat ramp nearby, service station nearby, 40-foot RV length limit, generators permitted, 14 day maximum stay.

Indian Creek: National Park Service campground about eight miles south of Mammoth Hot Springs Junction on Grand Loop Road, open June to September, 75 sites, $12 per night, water, vault toilets, 14 day stay limit. Ten sites can accommodate RVs up to 40 feet; 35 sites, 30 feet.

Lewis Lake: National Park Service campground ten miles south of West Thumb Junction on Lewis Lake, open June to November, 85 sites, $12 per night, 25-foot RV length limit, vault toilets, water, boat ramp, 14 day maximum stay.

Madison: concession-operated campground 14 miles east of West Entrance near Madison Junction, open May to October, 278 sites, $20.50 per night, flush toilets, dump station, 40-foot RV length limit, generators permitted, 14 day maximum stay.

Mammoth: National Park Service campground five miles south of North Entrance, open all year, 85 sites (most are pull-thru sites), $14 per night, drinking water, flush toilets, amphitheater, generators permitted, limited facilities in winter, 14 day maximum stay.

Norris: National Park Service campground one mile north of Norris Junction, open May to September, 116 sites, $14 per night, flush toilets, drinking water, generators permitted, 14 day maximum stay. Two sites can accommodate RVs up to 50 feet; five sites, 30 feet.

Pebble Creek: National Park Service campground seven miles south of Northeast Entrance and Silver Gate, open June to September, 27 sites (some pull-thru), $12 per night, vault toilets, drinking water, 14 day stay limit.

Slough Creek: National Park Service campground ten miles northeast of Tower Fall Junction, open June to October, 23 sites, $12 per night, water, vault toilets, 14 day maximum stay. There are 14 sites that can accommodate RVs up to 30 feet.

Tower Fall: National Park Service campground three miles southeast of Tower Junction, open May to September, 31 sites $12 per night, water, vault toilets, 30-foot RV length limit (hairpin curve in campground), limited groceries nearby, 14 day maximum.

Appendix A

America the Beautiful Passes

Annual Pass
The Annual Pass provides entrance or access to federally operated recreation sites where Entrance or Standard Amenity Fees are charged. The pass costs $80 and is valid for one year from the month of purchase. It admits the pass holder and three accompanying adults age 16 and older. The Annual Pass is honored at sites managed by the Forest Service, National Park Service, Fish and Wildlife Service, Bureau of Land Management, and Bureau of Reclamation. It does not reduce the use fees charged for camping, parking, etc.

The Annual Pass can be purchased by phone at 888-275-8747 ext. 1, online at http://store.usgs.gov/pass, or at any participating federal recreation site.

Senior Pass
The Senior Pass is available to U.S. Citizens and permanent residents who are 62 years and older. The pass provides entrance or access to recreation areas managed by the Forest Service, National Park Service, Fish and Wildlife Service, Bureau of Land Management, and Bureau of Reclamation. In addition, the Corps of Engineers and Tennessee Valley Authority may honor the Senior Pass. The Senior Pass also provides a discount on some Expanded Amenity Fees such as camping, parking, boat launching, and guided tours.

The cost of the Senior Pass is $10 and is valid for the lifetime of the pass owner. A Senior Pass can be obtained in person from a participating federal recreation site or office.

Access Pass
The Access Pass is a free, lifetime pass available to U.S. citizens or permanent residents of the United States that have been medically determined to have a permanent disability. The pass provides entrance or access to recreation areas managed by the Forest Service, National

Park Service, Fish and Wildlife Service, Bureau of Land Management, and Bureau of Reclamation. In addition, the Corps of Engineers and Tennessee Valley Authority may honor the Access Pass. The Access Pass also provides a discount on some Expanded Amenity Fees such as camping, parking, boat launching, and guided tours.

An Access Pass can be obtained in person from a participating federal recreation site or office. The pass is free and is valid for the lifetime of the pass owner. Proof of disability is required. Some examples of acceptable documentation include:

- Statement by a licensed physician

- Document issued by a Federal agency such as the Veteran's Administration, Social Security Disability Income, or Supplemental Security Income

- Document issued by a State agency such as a vocational rehabilitation agency.

Appendix B

Designation of National Park Service Units

The National Park Service manages nearly 400 areas (or units) covering more than 84 million acres in 49 states, the District of Columbia, and U.S. possessions. These areas include national parks, seashores, battlefields, and historic sites nationwide. They offer a wide variety of outdoor recreation and educational experiences for the visitor.

Although the National Park Service is best known for its great scenic parks, more than half of the areas preserve places that commemorate persons, events, and activities important in our nation's history. These range from archeological sites associated with prehistoric Indian civilizations to sites related to the lives of modern Americans.

The numerous designations within the National Park Service can be confusing to visitors. Listed below is a description of the different types of areas managed by the National Park Service.

- **National Park**: These are generally large natural places having a wide variety of attributes, at times including significant historic assets. Hunting, mining and consumptive activities are not authorized.

- **National Monument**: The Antiquities Act of 1906 authorized the President to declare by public proclamation landmarks, structures, and other objects of historic or scientific interest situated on lands owned or controlled by the government to be national monuments.

- **National Preserve**: National preserves are areas having characteristics associated with national parks, but in which Congress has permitted continued public hunting, trapping, oil/gas exploration and extraction. Many existing national preserves, without sport hunting, would qualify for national park designation.

- **National Historic Site**: Usually, a national historic site contains a single historical feature that was directly associated with its subject.

Derived from the Historic Sites Act of 1935, a number of historic sites were established by secretaries of the Interior, but most have been authorized by acts of Congress.

- **National Historical Park**: This designation generally applies to historic parks that extend beyond single properties or buildings.

- **National Memorial**: A national memorial is commemorative of a historic person or episode; it need not occupy a site historically connected with its subject.

- **National Battlefield**: This general title includes national battlefield, national battlefield park, national battlefield site, and national military park. In 1958, an NPS committee recommended national battlefield as the single title for all such park lands.

- **National Cemetery**: There are presently 14 national cemeteries in the National Park System, all of which are administered in conjunction with an associated unit and are not accounted for separately.

- **National Recreation Area**: Twelve national recreation areas (NRAs) in the system are centered on large reservoirs and emphasize water-based recreation. Five other NRAs are located near major population centers. Such urban parks combine scarce open spaces with the preservation of significant historic resources and important natural areas in a location that can provide outdoor recreation for large numbers of people.

- **National Seashore**: Ten national seashores have been established on the Atlantic, Gulf and Pacific coasts; some are developed and some relatively primitive. Hunting is allowed at many of these sites.

- **National Lakeshore**: National lakeshores, all on the Great Lakes, closely parallel the seashores in character and use.

- **National River**: There are several variations to this category: national river and recreation area, national scenic river, wild river, etc. The first was authorized in 1964 and others were established following passage of the Wild and Scenic Rivers Act of 1968.

- **National Parkway**: The title parkway refers to a roadway and the parkland paralleling the roadway. All were intended for scenic motoring along a protected corridor and often connect cultural sites.

- **National Trail**: National scenic trails and national historic trails are the titles given to these linear parklands (over 3,600 miles) authorized under the National Trails System Act of 1968.

- **Other Designations**: Some units of the National Park System bear unique titles or combinations of titles, like the White House and Prince William Forest Park.

Appendix C

Visiting Parks With Your Pets

Pets are generally permitted in National Park Service areas but must be restrained either on a leash not exceeding 6 feet in length, caged, or crated at all times. Park Superintendents and Managers have the discretion to further restrict areas open to pets (i.e. trails, buildings, and campgrounds may be off limits).

Restrictions on pets in parks are as much to protect your pet as to protect park resources. The following are some of the reasons parks give for regulating the presence of pets:

- When a loose pet chases a squirrel or raccoon, the wild animal's ability to survive is threatened, and when it is threatened, it may react aggressively.

- There is a strong possibility in parks such as Yellowstone that your pet could become prey for bear, coyote, owl, or other predators.

- There is a possibility of exchange of diseases between domestic animals and wildlife.

- Dogs, the most common traveling companion, are natural predators that may harass or even kill native wildlife that is protected within the park's boundaries.

- The "scent of a predator" that dogs leave behind can disrupt or alter the behavior of native animals.

- Pets may be hard to control, even on a leash, within confines of often narrow park trails and may trample or dig up fragile vegetation.

- Dog and cat feces add excessive nutrients and bacterial pollution to water, which decreases water quality and can also cause human health problems.

- Finally, lost domestic animals sometimes turn to preying on park wildlife and must be destroyed.

Some park webpages have lists of nearby kennels where you can leave your pet during your stay in the park. You can access information on the parks you plan to visit by going to the "Visit Your National Parks" website at www.nps.gov. It is always best to check with the park(s) you are planning to visit for specific information and restrictions for pets.

Appendix D

Free Camping Areas

Following is a list that identifies campgrounds in National Park Service areas where free camping is available. For camping areas accessible only by walking, hiking, biking, or boating you will find the term "no drive-up" after the campground name. This list does not include backcountry camping opportunities, which are generally free although there may be a charge for a permit.

ALASKA
Glacier Bay National Park & Preserve
- Bartlett Cove (no drive-up)

Kenai Fjords National Park
- Exit Glacier (no drive-up)

ARIZONA
Navajo National Monument
- Canyon View
- Sunset View

ARKANSAS
Buffalo National River
- Maumee South
- Spring Creek
- Woolum

CALIFORNIA
Death Valley National Park
- Emigrant
- Mahogany Flat
- Thorndike
- Wildrose

Golden Gate National Recreation Area
- Bicentennial (no drive-up)
- Hawkcamp (no drive-up)
- Haypress (no drive-up)

COLORADO

Curecanti National Recreation Area
- Gateview

Dinosaur National Monument
- Rainbow Park
- Split Mountain

FLORIDA

Big Cypress National Preserve
- Bear Island
- Burns Lake
- Mitchell's Landing
- Pinecrest

HAWAII

Haleakala National Park
- Hosmer Grove
- Kipahulu

Hawaii Volcanoes National Park
- Namakanipaio
- Kulanaokuaiki

MICHIGAN

Isle Royale National Park
- All 36 campgrounds (no drive-up)

MINNESOTA

Grand Portage National Monument
- Fort Charlotte (no drive-up)

Voyageurs National Park
- All campsites are free (no drive-up)

MISSISSIPPI
Natchez Trace Parkway
- Jeff Busby
- Meriwether Lewis
- Rocky Springs

MONTANA
Bighorn Canyon National Recreation Area
- Afterbay
- Black Canyon
- Horseshoe Bend
- Medicine Creek
- Trail Creek

NEVADA
Great Basin National Park
- Strawberry Creek

NEW MEXICO
El Malpais National Monument
- Joe Skeen

SOUTH CAROLINA
Congaree National Park
- Longleaf

SOUTH DAKOTA
Badlands National Park
- Sage Creek

TEXAS
Lake Meredith National Recreation Area
- Blue Creek Bridge
- Blue West
- Bugbee
- Cedar Canyon
- Chimney Hollow
- Fritch Fortress
- Harbor Bay

- McBride Canyon
- Plum Creek
- Rosita
- Sanford-Yake

Padre Island National Seashore
- North Beach
- South Beach
- Yarborough Pass

UTAH
Capitol Reef National Park
- Cathedral Valley
- Cedar Mesa

Zion National Park
- Lava Point

WASHINGTON
Lake Roosevelt National Recreation Area
- Crystal Cove (no drive-up)
- Detillion (no drive-up)
- Enterprise (no drive-up)
- Goldsmith (no drive-up)
- Halverson Canyon (no drive-up)
- Penix (no drive-up)
- Plum Point (no drive-up)
- Ponderosa (no drive-up)
- Sterling Point (no drive-up)
- Summer Island (no drive-up)

Mount Rainier National Park
- Ipsut Creek (no drive-up)
- Mowich Lake (no drive-up)

North Cascades National Park
- Gorge Lake
- Hozomeen

WEST VIRGINIA
New River Gorge National River
- Army Camp
- Brooklyn
- Glade Creek
- Grandview Sandbar
- Stone Cliff
- Thayer
- War Ridge/Backus Mountain

Appendix E

RV Camping Areas

Use the following list as a quick reference for locating RV accessible campgrounds throughout the National Park Service areas. Refer back to the park for the full listing with more details about the campground.

Maximum lengths for trailers, campers, and motorhomes vary from park to park. The average maximum length permitted is 27 feet, but some parks can accommodate RVs up to 40 feet or more in length.

You should always check with your favorite park for their specific maximum lengths and available facilities so you won't be disappointed when you arrive.

ALASKA
Denali National Park & Preserve
- Riley Creek: all year, 147 sites, $22-$28, 40-foot limit.
- Savage River: May-Sep, 33 sites, $22-$28, 40-foot limit.
- Teklanika River: May-Sep, 53 sites, $16, 40-foot limit.

Klondike Gold Rush National Historical Park
- Dyea: open when free of snow, 22 rustic sites, $10, no hookups.

ARIZONA
Canyon de Chelly National Monument
- Cottonwood: all year, 90 sites, $10, 40-foot limit.

Chiricahua National Monument
- Bonita Canyon: all year, 22 sites, $12, no hookups, 29-foot limit.

Grand Canyon National Park
- Desert View: May-Oct, 50 sites, $12, no hookups, 30-foot limit.
- Mather: all year, 318 sites, $15-$18, no hookups, 30-foot limit.

- Trailer Village: all year, 78 sites, $35, full hookups, 50-foot limit.
- North Rim: May-Oct, 81 sites, $18-$25, no hookups.

Navajo National Monument
- Canyon View: Apr-Sep, 16 sites, no fee, no hookups.
- Sunset View: all year, 31 sites, no fee, no hookups, 28-foot limit.

Organ Pipe Cactus National Monument
- Alamo Canyon: all year, 4 sites, $8, motorhomes and trailers prohibited.
- Twin Peaks: all year, 208 sites, $12, 40-foot limit.

Sunset Crater Volcano National Monument
- Bonito: May-Oct, 44 sites, $18, no hookups, 42-foot limit.

ARKANSAS
Buffalo National River
- Buffalo Point: all year, 83 sites with water and electric, $17, 31-foot limit.
- Erbie: all year, 14 sites, $10 (Apr-Oct, no fees Nov-Mar).
- Spring Creek: all year, 14 sites, no fee.
- Tyler Bend: all year, 28 sites, $12 (no fees Nov-Mar). No hookups, 28-foot limit.

Hot Springs National Park
- Gulpha Gorge: all year, 43 sites, $10 no hookup sites, $24 full hookup sites.

CALIFORNIA
Death Valley National Park
- Furnace Creek: all year, 136 sites, $12-$18, no hookups, 35-foot limit.
- Mesquite Spring: all year, 30 sites, $12, 35-foot limit.
- Stovepipe Wells: Oct-Apr, 190 sites, $12, 35-foot limit.
- Sunset: Oct-Apr, 270 sites, $12, 40-foot limit.
- Texas Spring: Oct-Apr, 92 sites, $14, 35-foot limit.
- Wildrose: all year, 23 sites, no fee, 25-foot limit.

Devil's Postpile National Monument
- Devil's Postpile: Jul-Sep, 21 sites, $14.

Joshua Tree National Park
- Belle: all year, 18 sites, $10, no hookups.
- Black Rock: all year, 100 sites, $15, no hookups, 35-foot limit.
- Cottonwood: all year, 62 sites, $15, no hookups.
- Hidden Valley: all year, 39 sites, $10, no hookups, 25-foot limit.
- Indian Cove: all year, 101 sites, $15, no hookups.
- Jumbo Rocks: all year, 124 sites, $10, no hookups.
- Ryan: all year, 31 sites, $10, no hookups.
- White Tank: all year, 15 sites, $10, no hookups, 25-foot limit.

Lassen Volcanic National Park
- Butte Lake: Jun-Oct, 101 sites, $16, no hookups, 45-foot limit.
- Crags: Jun-Sep, 45 sites, $12, 45-foot limit, no hookups.
- Manzanita Lake: May-Oct, 179 sites, $18, no hookups, 45-foot limit.
- Summit Lake North: Jun-Sep, 46 sites, $18, no hookups, 45-foot limit.
- Summit Lake South: Jun-Oct, 48 sites, $16, no hookups.

Lava Beds National Monument
- Indian Well: all year, 43 sites, $10, 30-foot limit.

Mojave National Preserve
- Hole-in-the-Wall: all year, 35 sites, $12.

Pinnacles National Monument
- Pinnacles: all year, 36 sites with electric hookups, $36.

Redwood National and State Parks
- Elk Prairie: all year, 75 sites, $35, no hookups, 27-foot limit.
- Gold Bluffs Beach: Apr-Sep, 26 sites, $35, no hookups, 24-foot limit.
- Jedediah Smith: all year, 86 sites, $35, no hookups, 36-foot limit.
- Mill Creek: May-Sep, 145 sites, $35, no hookups, 31-foot limit.

Santa Monica Mountains National Recreation Area
- Canyon Family Camp: all year, 135 sites, $45, 31-foot limit.
- Big Sycamore Canyon Family Camp: all year, 58 sites, $45, 31-foot limit.
- Thornhill Broome Family Camp: all year, 68 sites, $35.
- Malibu Creek Family Camp: all year, 62 sites, $45, 30-foot limit.

Sequoia & Kings Canyon National Parks

Campgrounds in Kings Canyon National Park
- Azalea: all year, 110 sites, $18, limited RV space, no hookups.
- Canyon View: open as needed May-Oct, 23 sites, $18, no hookups.
- Crystal Springs: May-Sep, 36 sites, $18, no hookups.
- Moraine: open as needed May-Oct, 120 sites, $18, no hookups.
- Sentinel: May-Sep, 82 sites, $18, no hookups.
- Sheep Creek: open as needed May-Oct, 111 sites, $18, no hookups.
- Sunset: May-Sep, 157 sites, $18, no hookups.

Campgrounds in Sequoia National Park
- Dorst Creek: Jun-Sep, 218 sites, $20, no hookups.
- Lodgepole: Apr-Oct, 214 sites, $20, no hookups.
- Potwisha: all year, 42 sites, $18, no hookups.

Whiskeytown National Recreation Area
- Brandy Creek: all year, 37 sites, $14, 35-foot limit.
- Oak Bottom: all year, 22 sites, $18.

Yosemite National Park
- Bridalveil Creek: Jul-Sep, 110 sites, $14, no hookups, 35-foot limit.
- Crane Flat: Jun-Oct, 166 sites, $20, no hookups, 40-foot limit.
- Hodgdon Meadow: all year, 105 sites, $20, no hookups, 40-foot limit.
- Lower Pines: Mar-Oct, 60 sites, $20, no hookups, 40-foot limit.
- North Pines: Apr-Nov, 81 sites, $20, no hookups, 40-foot limit.
- Porcupine Flat: Jul-Oct, 52 sites, $10, no hookups, 24-foot limit.
- Tamarack Flat: Jun-Oct, 52 sites, $10, no hookups, no trailers or large RVs.
- Tuolumne Meadows: Jul-Sep, 304 sites, $20, no hookups, 35-foot limit.
- Upper Pines: all year, 238 sites, $20, no hookups, 35-foot limit.
- Wawona: all year, 93 sites, $20, no hookups, 35-foot limit.
- White Wolf: Jun-Sep, 74 sites, $14, no hookups, 27-foot limit.

COLORADO

Black Canyon of the Gunnison National Park
- North Rim: open spring to fall, 13 sites, $12, no hookups, 35-foot limit.
- South Rim: Loop A all year; Loop B & C spring to fall, 88 sites, $12 (electric in Loop B, $18), 35-foot limit.

Colorado National Monument
- Saddlehorn: all year, 80 sites, $20.

Curecanti National Recreation Area
- Cimarron: spring to fall, 21 sites (5 pull-thru), $12.
- Dry Gulch: spring to fall, 9 sites, $12.
- East Portal: spring to fall, 15 sites, $12, 22-foot limit.
- Elk Creek: all year, 160 sites (20 pull-thru), $12 (electric in Loop D, $18).
- Gateview: open spring to fall, 6 sites, no fee.
- Lake Fork: open spring to fall, 90 sites, $12.
- Ponderosa: open spring to fall, 28 sites, $12.
- Red Creek: open spring to fall, 1 site, $12.
- Stevens Creek: open spring to fall, 53 sites, $12.

Dinosaur National Monument
- Gates of Lodore: all year, 17 sites, $8, 35-foot limit.
- Green River: Apr-Oct, 80 sites, $12, 35-foot limit.

Great Sand Dunes National Park & Preserve
- Pinyon Flats: all year, 88 sites, $20, 35-foot limit.

Mesa Verde National Park
- Morefield: May-Oct, 267 sites (15 with full hookups), $26 and up.

Rocky Mountain National Park
- Aspenglen: May-Sep, 54 sites, $20, no hookups, 30-foot limit.
- Glacier Basin: Jun-Sep, 150 sites, $20, no hookups, 35-foot limit.
- Moraine Park: all year, 245 sites, $20, no hookups, 40-foot limit.
- Timber Creek: all year, 98 sites, $20, no hookups, 30-foot limit.

FLORIDA
Big Cypress National Preserve
- Bear Island: all year, 40 sites, no fee, primitive campground.
- Burns Lake: Aug-Jan, 14 sites, no fee, primitive campground.
- Midway: all year, 26 sites with electric hookups, $19.
- Mitchell's Landing: all year, 15 sites, no fee, primitive campground.
- Monument Lake: Aug-Apr, 26 sites, $16, no hookups.
- Pinecrest: all year, 10 sites, no fee, primitive campground.

Everglades National Park
- Flamingo: all year, 234 sites (41 with hookups), $30.
- Long Pine Key: all year, 108 sites, $16, no hookups, 36-foot limit.

Gulf Islands National Seashore
- Davis Bayou: all year, 51 sites with electric & water, $16, 45-foot limit.
- Fort Pickens: all year, 180 sites with electric & water, $20.

IDAHO
Craters of the Moon National Monument
- Lava Flow: May-Oct, 51 sites, $6-$10.

INDIANA
Indiana Dunes National Lakeshore
- Dunewood: Apr-Oct, 53 sites, $15, no hookups.

KENTUCKY
Cumberland Gap National Historical Park
- Wilderness Road: campground is located in Virginia, open all year, 160 sites, $12 (41 sites with 30 & 50 amp electric, $17).

Mammoth Cave National Park
- Mammoth Cave: all year, 105 sites, $17, no hookups.

MAINE
Acadia National Park
- Blackwoods: all year, 306 sites, $20, 35-foot limit.
- Seawall: May-Sep, 214 sites, $20, 35-foot limit.

MARYLAND
Assateague Island National Seashore
- Developed: all year, 90 sites, $20-$25, 40-foot limit.

Catoctin Mountain Park
- Owens Creek: May-Nov, 50 sites, $20, 50-foot limit (trailers 22 feet).

Chesapeake & Ohio Canal National Historical Park
- Fifteen Mile Creek: all year, 10 sites, $10, 20-foot limit.
- McCoys Ferry: all year, 14 sites, $10, 20-foot limit.
- Spring Gap: all year, 20 sites, $10, 20-foot limit.

Greenbelt Park
- Greenbelt Park: all year, 174 sites, $16, no hookups.

MICHIGAN
Pictured Rocks National Lakeshore
- Hurricane River: May-Oct, 21 sites, $14, 36-foot limit.
- Little Beaver Lake: May-Oct, 8 sites, $14, 36-foot limit.
- Twelvemile Beach: May-Oct, 36 sites, $14-$16, 36-foot limit.

Sleeping Bear Dunes National Lakeshore
- D.H. Day: Apr-Nov, 88 sites, $12.
- Platte River: all year, 149 sites (96 with 30-amp electric), $16-$21.

MISSISSIPPI
Natchez Trace Parkway
- Jeff Busby: in Mississippi, all year, 18 sites, no fee.
- Meriwether Lewis: in Tennessee, all year, 32 sites, no fee.
- Rocky Springs: in Mississippi, all year, 22 sites, no fee.

MISSOURI
Ozark National Scenic Riverways
- Alley Spring: all year, 162 sites (some with 50 amp electric), $17-$20.
- Big Spring: all year, 123 sites (some with electric), $17-$20.
- Powder Mill: all year, 8 sites, $17, no hookups.
- Pulltite: all year, 55 sites, $17, no hookups.

- Round Spring: all year, 60 sites (some with 50 amp electric), $17-$20.
- Two Rivers: all year, 19 sites, $17.

MONTANA
Bighorn Canyon National Recreation Area
- Afterbay: all year, 28 sites, no fee.
- Horseshoe Bend: in Wyoming, open all year, 29 sites without hookups (free), 19 sites with hookups ($15).
- Trail Creek: in Wyoming, all year, 10 sites, no fee, 16-foot limit.

Glacier National Park
- Apgar: May-Oct, 194 sites, $20, no hookups, 40-foot limit.
- Avalanche: Jun-Sep, 87 sites, $20, no hookups, 26-foot limit.
- Fish Creek: Jun-Sep, 178 sites, $23, no hookups, 35-foot limit.
- Many Glacier: May-Sep, 110 sites, $20, no hookups, 35-foot limit.
- Rising Sun: May-Sep, 83 sites, $20, no hookups, 25-foot limit.
- Sprague Creek: May-Sep, 25 sites, $20, no hookups, no towed units.
- Saint Mary: May-Sep, 148 sites, $23, no hookups, 35-foot limit.
- Two Medicine: May-Sep, 99 sites, $20, no hookups, 32-foot limit.

NEVADA
Great Basin National Park
- Baker Creek: May-Oct, 34 sites, some pull-thru, $12, 30-foot limit.
- Lower Lehman Creek: all year, 11 sites, some pull-thru, $12, 42-foot limit.
- Upper Lehman Creek: Apr-Oct, 22 sites, $12, 36-foot limit.
- Wheeler Peak: Jun-Oct, 37 sites, $12, 24-foot limit.

Lake Mead National Recreation Area
- Boulder Beach: all year, 154 sites, $10.
- Callville Bay: all year, 80 sites, $10.
- Cottonwood Cove: all year, 145 sites, $10.
- Echo Bay: all year, 166 sites, $10.
- Katherine Landing: all year, 173 sites, $10.
- Las Vegas Bay: all year, 89 sites, $10.
- Temple Bar: all year, 153 sites, $10.

NEW MEXICO

Bandelier National Monument

- Juniper: all year, 94 sites, $12, 41-foot limit.

Chaco Culture National Historical Park

- Gallo: all year, 49 sites, $10, 35-foot limit.

El Malpais National Monument

- Joe Skeen: all year, 10 sites, no fee, 50-foot limit.

El Morro National Monument

- El Morro: all year, 9 sites, $5, no hookups, 27-foot limit.

NORTH CAROLINA

Blue Ridge Parkway

Campgrounds in Virginia

- Otter Creek: May-Oct, 24 sites, $16, 30-foot limit.
- Peaks of Otter: May-Oct, 59 sites, $16, 30-foot limit.
- Roanoke Mountain: May-Oct, 30 sites, $16, 30-foot limit.
- Rocky Knob: May-Oct, 28 sites, $16, 30-foot limit.

Campgrounds in North Carolina

- Doughton Park: May-Oct, 25 sites, $16, 30-foot limit.
- Julian Price Memorial Park: May-Oct, 68 sites, $16, 30-foot limit.
- Linville Falls: May-Oct, 20 sites, $16, 30-foot limit.
- Crabtree Meadows: May-Oct, 22 sites, $16, 30-foot limit.
- Mount Pisgah: May-Oct, 67 sites, $16, 30-foot limit.

Cape Hatteras National Seashore

- Cape Point: Jun-Sep, 202 sites, $20.
- Frisco: Apr-Oct, 127 sites, $20.
- Ocracoke: Apr-Oct, 136 sites, $23.
- Oregon Inlet: Apr-Oct, 120 sites, $20.

NORTH DAKOTA

Theodore Roosevelt National Park

- Cottonwood: all year, 76 sites (some pull-thrus), $10.
- Juniper: all year, 50 sites (some pull-thrus), $10.

OKLAHOMA
Chickasaw National Recreation Area
- Buckhorn: Campsites situated within four loops.
  Loop A: May-Sep, 20 sites, $16.
  Loop B: May-Sep, 5 sites, $16.
  Loop C: Mar-Dec, 27 sites (17 with electric), $16-$24.
  Loop D: all year, 37 sites (24 with electric), $16-$24.
- Cold Springs, May-Sep, 63 sites, $14, 20-foot limit.
- Guy Sandy: May-Aug, 40 sites, $14.
- Rock Creek: all year, 105 sites (mostly tent-only, some for RVs), $14.
- The Point: 58 sites in two loops.
  Lower Loop: all year, 37 sites (9 with electric), $16-$22.
  Upper Loop: all year, 21 sites (12 with electric), $16-$22.

OREGON
Crater Lake National Park
- Mazama: Jun-Sep, 212 sites (some with electric), $21 to $29.

PENNSYLVANIA
Delaware Water Gap National Recreation Area
- Dingmans: Jan-Dec, 133 sites, $32-$37.

SOUTH DAKOTA
Badlands National Park
- Cedar Pass: all year, 96 sites, $16-$28.

Wind Cave National Park
- Elk Mountain: all year, 75 sites (25 pull-thru), $12.

TENNESSEE
Big South Fork National River & Recreation Area
- Alum Ford: in Kentucky, all year, 6 primitive sites, $5.
- Bandy Creek: all year, 96 sites with water & electric, $22.
- Blue Heron: in Kentucky, Apr-Nov, 45 sites with water & electric, $17.

Great Smoky Mountains National Park

Campgrounds in Tennessee
- Abrams Creek: May-Oct, 16 sites, $14, 12-foot limit.
- Cades Cove: all year, 159 sites, $17-$20, 40-foot limit.
- Cosby: Apr-Oct, 165 sites, $14, 25-foot limit.
- Elkmont: Mar-Nov, 220 sites, $17-$23, 35-foot limit.
- Look Rock: May-Oct, 68 sites, $14, no length limit.

Campgrounds in North Carolina
- Balsam Mountain: May-Oct, 46 sites, $14, 30-foot limit.
- Cataloochee: Mar-Oct, 27 sites, $20, 31-foot limit.
- Deep Creek: Apr-Oct, 92 sites, $17, 26-foot limit.
- Smokemont: all year, 142 sites, $17-$20, 35-foot limit.

TEXAS

Amistad National Recreation Area
- 277 North: all year, 17 sites, $4, no hookups, no RV length limit.
- Governors Landing: all year, 15 sites, $8, no hookups, 28-foot limit.
- Rough Canyon: all year, 4 sites, $4, no hookups, no RV length limit.
- San Pedro: all year, 35 sites, $4, no hookups, no RV length limit.
- Spur 406: all year, 8 sites, $4, no hookups, no RV length limit.

Big Bend National Park
- Chisos Basin: all year, 60 sites, $14, 24-foot limt (20 feet for trailers).
- Cottonwood: all year, 31 sites, $14, 30-foot limit.
- Rio Grande Village: all year, 100 sites (some pull-thrus), $14.
- Rio Grande Village RV Park: all year, 25 sites (full hookups), $33.

Guadalupe Mountains National Park
- Dog Canyon: all year, 4 sites, $8, no hookups.
- Pine Springs: all year, 19 sites, $8, no hookups.

Lake Meredith National Recreation Area
- Blue Creek Bridge: all year, no designated sites, no fee.
- Blue West: all year, designated sites, no fee.
- Bugbee: all year, no designated sites, no fee.
- Cedar Canyon: all year, no designated sites, no fee.
- Chimney Hollow: all year, no designated sites, no fee.
- Fritch Fortress: all year, individual campsites, no fee.

- Harbor Bay: all year, no designated sites, no fee.
- McBride Canyon: all year, no designated sites, no fee.
- Plum Creek: all year, no designated sites, no fee.
- Rosita: all year, no designated sites, no fee.
- Sanford-Yake: all year, individual sites, no fee.

Padre Island National Seashore
- Bird Island Basin: all year, primitive camping open to RVs and tents, $5.
- Malaquite: all year, 42 sites, $8, no hookups.
- North Beach: all year, primitive camping open to RVs and tents, no fee.
- South Beach: all year, no designated sites, no fees.

UTAH
Arches National Park
- Devils Garden: all year, 50 sites, $20, 30-foot limit.

Bryce Canyon National Park
- North: all year, 99 sites (some pull-thrus), $15, 30-foot limit.
- Sunset: spring to fall, 100 sites, $15, 45-foot limit.

Canyonlands National Park
- Squaw Flat: all year, 26 sites, $15, 28-foot limit.
- Willow Flat: all year, 12 sites, $10, 28-foot limit.

Capitol Reef National Park
- Cedar Mesa: all year, 5 sites, primitive camping, no fee.
- Fruita: all year, 71 sites, $10.

Cedar Breaks National Monument
- Point Supreme: Jun-Sep, 28 sites, $14, 35-foot limit.

Glen Canyon National Recreation Area
- Bullfrog RV Park (Painted Hills): in Utah, all year, 24 sites with full hookups, $50, 50-foot limit.
- Halls Crossing: in Utah, all year, 24 sites with full hookups, $48, 60-foot limit.
- Lees Ferry: in Arizona, all year, 54 sites, $12, 35-foot limit.
- Wahweap: in Arizona, all year, 139 full hookup sites, $48.

Hovenweep National Monument
- Hovenweep: all year, 31 sites, $10, 36-foot limit.

Natural Bridges National Monument
- Natural Bridges: all year, 13 sites, $10, 26-foot limit.

Zion National Park
- Lava Point: Jun-Oct, 6 primitive sites, no fee, 19-foot limit.
- South: Mar-Oct, 127 sites, $16.
- Watchman: all year, 95 sites with electric, $18-$20.

VIRGINIA
Prince William Forest Park
- Oak Ridge: all year, 100 sites, $20, 32-foot limit.
- Prince William Forest RV Campground: all year, 72 sites (full hookups available), $31-$34, 35-foot limit.

Shenandoah National Park
- Big Meadows: Mar-Nov, 217 sites (some pull-thrus), $20.
- Lewis Mountain: Apr-Oct, 31 sites, $15.
- Loft Mountain: May-Oct, 219 sites (some pull-thrus), $15.
- Mathews Arm: May-Oct, 179 sites (some pull-thrus), $14.

WASHINGTON
Lake Roosevelt National Recreation Area
- Evans: all year, 43 sites, $10.
- Fort Spokane: all year, 67 sites, $10.
- Gifford: all year, 42 sites, $10.
- Haag Cove: all year, 16 sites, $10.
- Hawk Creek: all year, 21 sites, $10.
- Hunters: all year, 39 sites, $10.
- Jones Bay: all year, 9 sites, $10.
- Kamloops: all year, 17 sites, $10.
- Keller Ferry: all year, 55 sites, $10.
- Kettle Falls: all year, 76 sites, $10.
- Kettle River: all year, 13 sites, $10.
- Marcus Island: all year, 27 sites, $10.
- North Gorge: all year, 12 sites, $10.
- Porcupine Bay: all year, 31 sites, $10.
- Snag Cove: all year, 9 sites, $10.
- Spring Canyon: all year, 87 sites, $10.

Mount Rainier National Park
- Cougar Rock: May-Oct, 173 sites, $12-$15, 35-foot limit (trailers, 27 feet).
- Ohanapecosh: May-Oct, 188 sites, $12-$15, 32-foot limit (trailers, 27 feet).
- White River: Jun-Sep, 112 sites, $12.

North Cascades National Park
- Colonial Creek: May-Oct, 142 sites, $12.
- Goodell Creek: all year, 21 sites, $10. No large RVs.
- Gorge Lake: all year, primitive camping, 6 sites, no fee.
- Hozomeen: Jun-Oct, 75 sites, no fee.
- Newhalem Creek: May-Sep, 111 sites, $12, Large RVs can be accommodated.

Olympic National Park
- Altaire: May-Sep, 30 sites, $12, 35-foot limit.
- Elwha: all year, 40 sites, $12, 35-foot limit.
- Fairholme: Apr-Oct, 88 sites (some pull-thrus), $12, 21-foot limit.
- Graves Creek: all year, 30 sites, $12, 21-foot limit.
- Heart O' the Hills: all year, 105 sites, $12, 35-foot limit.
- Hoh: all year, 88 sites, $12, 21-foot limit.
- Kalaloch: all year, 170 sites, $18, 35-foot limit.
- Mora: all year, 94 sites (some pull-thrus), $12, 35-foot limit.
- Ozette: all year, 15 sites, $12, 21-foot limit.
- Sol Duc: all year, 82 sites, $14, 35-foot limit.
- South Beach: May-Sep, 50 sites, $10, 35-foot limit.
- Staircase: all year, 47 sites, $12, 35-foot limit.

WEST VIRGINIA
New River Gorge National River
- Army Camp: all year, 11 sites, no fee.
- Brooklyn: all year, 1 site, no fee.
- Glade Creek: all year, 5 sites, no fee, no large RVs.
- Grandview Sandbar: all year, 10 sites, no fee, no large RVs.
- Stone Cliff: all year, 1 site, no fee.
- War Ridge/Backus Mountain: all year, 8 sites, no fee, no large RVs.

WYOMING

Devils Tower National Monument
- Belle Fourche: spring to fall, 50 sites, $12, 35-foot limit.

Grand Teton National Park
- Colter Bay: May-Sep, 350 sites, $20.50.
- Colter Bay RV Park: May-Sep, 112 sites (full hookups, some pull-thrus), $57.
- Flagg Ranch: Jun-Sep, 100 sites (full hookups, 20 amp, pull-thru), $64.
- Gros Ventre: May-Oct, 350 sites, $20.50.
- Lizard Creek: Jun-Sep, 60 sites, $20.50, 30-foot limit.
- Signal Mountain: May-Oct, 86 sites, $20.50, 30-foot limit.

Yellowstone National Park, 225
- Bridge Bay: May-Sep, 432 sites, $20.50, 40-foot limit.
- Canyon: Jun-Sep, 273 sites, $25, 40-foot limit.
- Fishing Bridge RV Park: May-Sep, 346 sites (full hookups), $45, 40-foot limit.
- Grant Village: Jun-Sep, 430 sites, $25, 40-foot limit.
- Indian Creek: Jun-Sep, 75 sites, $12, RV length limit 30 to 40 feet.
- Lewis Lake: Jun-Nov, 85 sites, $12, 25-foot limit.
- Madison: May-Oct, 278 sites, $20.50, 40-foot limit.
- Mammoth: all year, 85 sites (some pull-thrus), $14.
- Norris: May-Sep, 116 sites, $14, 2 sites can fit RV up to 50 feet; 5 sites, 30 feet.
- Pebble Creek: Jun-Sep, 27 sites (some pull-thrus), $12.
- Slough Creek: Jun-Oct, 23 sites, $12, 30-foot limit.
- Tower Fall: May-Sep, 31 sites, $12, 30-foot limit.

Index